daddy, daughters, & devotions

stories of life & love to refocus and refuel your purpose

SPECIAL EDITION

—LABRYANT FRIEND—

A 35 Day Devotional to Encourage Your Daily Walk with God

Limits of Liability and Disclaimer of Warranty

The author and publisher shall not be liable for your misuse of this material. This book is strictly for informational and educational purposes. The purpose of this book is to educate and entertain. The author and/or publisher do not guarantee that anyone following these techniques, suggestions, tips, ideas, or strategies will become successful. The author and/or publisher shall have neither liability nor responsibility to anyone with respect to any loss or damage caused, or alleged to be caused, directly or indirectly by the information contained in this book.

Views expressed in this publication do not necessarily reflect the views of the publisher.

Printed in the United States of America
Cover Design by Justin Foster
Photography by Jeremy Marc Anthony McBean

ISBN: 978-0-9982523-6-0
Keen Vision Publishing
www.keen-vision.com

–DEDICATION–

To my mother, *Phyllis Friend*, who passed away one week before the initial release of Daddy, Daughters, and Devotions, I am forever indebted to you for the seed of childlike faith you instilled. I love and miss you immensely.

To *Phineka Friend*, thank you for sharing the highs and lows of life with me. Without question, I don't have a clue of what I would do without you. I love you!

To the *Friendlettes*, you make this possible. You supply me with stories that keep life exciting. For your own little unique personalities, thank you!

To *Theodus Friend*, thank you for still believing in this "knucklehead" and knowing what is on the inside of me. Your faith in me pushes me beyond my boundaries.

–ABOUT THE AUTHOR–

Pastor LaBryant Friend has traveled throughout the nation and abroad sharing the heart of the King and His Kingdom. He has served in ministry for 16 years and has lead in various capacities of pastoral leadership – from Youth Pastor to Senior Pastor. His academic matriculation, which features graduate and seminary level experience, is balanced by his practical application and vivid engagement of the Word of God. He is a sought after conference speaker and uses every opportunity to bring truth and clarity into the lives of believers. As a family man, he is married to Phineka Friend and they together share in the joy of raising four beautiful daughters.

–CONTENTS–

Dedication ... iii

Introduction ... 1

Introducing My Daughters ... 3

Deal with It ... 9

The Open Door ... 17

Making Adjustments ... 25

The "Bandache" ... 33

Praying God's Will ... 41

Learning God's Voice ... 49

Do We Really Need All This? ... 57

I Need More Time ... 65

The Search ... 73

Who are You Imitating? ... 81

Keep Moving ... 89

From the Inside Out ... 97

You're Worth Something ... 105

The Boyfriend Saga ... 113

Cleaning up the Mess ... 121

Let's Work Together ... 129

Addicted No More ... 137

It's a New Day ... 145

What's in Your Heart? ... 153

I Need You ... 161

Anywhere, but Backward 169
Pick Me Up 177
Following the Right Steps 185
Let It Go 193
Living in Purpose 201
Pushing Through the Pain 209
You've Outgrown This 217
The Trust Factor 225
The Search 233
You Are a Survivor 241
Praying for Purpose 249
Help! I Have Ants in My Pants! 257
Broken, but Available 265
It Wasn't Me! 273
Starting Over 281

—INTRODUCTION—

Since our days in Tulsa, OK, I've wondered about the first book I would write. While I was away as a guest speaker at a youth conference in Detroit, Michigan, a pastor prophesied over my ability to write and tell stories. He spoke of the books that would come out of me and how those books would bless many because of the way God spoke to my heart.

At the time, I had not considered being a writer. Heck, I was just trying to rush through writing papers to finish grad school! I had no intention of writing any more for a season, but the more I mulled over the prophecy, the more it made sense. I realized that what God blessed me with on a weekly basis could bless the lives of others as well.

Four years later, my family had expanded from three to six members. Through that growth, I learned so much about myself, life, and more importantly, fatherhood. At the beginning of our marriage, Phineka and I had been immediately thrust into the role of parents. When we started our life together, Ashriel was already a happy part of the equation. With kids all over the house, I vowed to be the best father I could be so my children would always have a strong perception of God, men, and family.

Being an active father comes with a myriad of stories and lessons. The girls learn from us daily, but they also teach us so much about life, purpose, and the presence of God in all we do. As I sat down and began to think of all the stories we'd posted via social media, I gained the confidence to write this book.

Every family has its own story. Though there may be many similarities, each family has its own unique features and attributes. With that in mind, Phineka and I decided it was time to share our life stories with the world. As you read this book, know that it isn't just geared toward dads. On the contrary, it is for anyone who desires to jump on the path of discovering the power of purpose in their lives.

This book is extremely practical. As you read each devotional, my prayer is that you will be able to take away a story and Scripture that you can apply to your own life. By the end of this devotional, you will have gained a renewed sense of purpose in life.

Enjoy the stories! As you read each one, allow God to speak to your heart. I pray that as you read Daddy, Daughters, & Devotions, your purpose will be revealed and restored. Your life was created with greatness. Allow the purpose of God to be revealed in your life through this daddy, these daughters, and these devotions!

—INTRODUCING MY DAUGHTERS—

ASHRIEL

Covenant of God; God has made me happy.

At eleven years old, Ashriel is the oldest of our tribe. As of now, she is still the daughter with the most personality. She is a social butterfly and rarely finds herself in an environment where she does not easily adapt well to people. Her name is a reminder that in every circumstance, God is a Keeper of His promises and has the ability to keep His happiness in our hearts.

In our home, Ashriel is the "mother hen." Her sisters often look to her for direction, approval, and nurturing. She shoulders a tremendous amount of responsibility for us in the way she helps care for her sisters. As the preteen in our home, her life changes have only intensified the way her sisters look to her for understanding and guidance.

Ashriel has the gift of gab. She can start full conversations with people she has never met and quickly gain "best friends." Even in our relocation to Georgia, she is very often the center of attention, the class pet, and the defender of the innocent at her school. Without question, she has a genuine heart for people. She takes great joy in helping others and prides herself on rooting for the "underdog." She has built a reputation as one who loves showering others with compliments. She always finds a way to compliment the smallest thing about anyone.

Being the oldest child comes with the disadvantage of having to share the attention. Ashriel was our only child for five years. Time has taught her that we need to balance our time and attention with her. She is, without question, the apple of my eye and the greatest oldest daughter we could ever desire.

LONDYN

A strong fortress and ruler.

Londyn was the second addition to the Friend Tribe. At the age of six, she is evolving into her little personality and discovering her individuality as a little girl. She is the observant introvert of the four. She never misses one thing that transpires, peers into every situation with the eyes of wisdom, and showers us with reflections that are very often beyond her years. Even her silence speaks volumes.

Londyn is the reason I determined it was time to finish this book. Once she started preschool, she became a Facebook and Socialcam sensation because of her boyfriend, Alex. We shared her discovery of personality, life, and love of people with the world. Now that we are releasing the revisions, thankfully, all boyfriends have been removed from her life.

As the first middle child, Londyn takes several of her cues from Ashriel. She has a strong, independent nature. She is a creature of habit who doesn't like her routines to be broken. Whereas Ashriel gravitates to people, Londyn is much more cautious and discerning of people and their personalities. She will observe the development of situations from a distance before she decides to participate.

Londyn is the "diva" of the bunch. She always wants her hair done perfectly. Heck, she even wants her pajamas to match! She won't do anything that could potentially mess up her outfit or how she looks. At home, she loves to be the center of attention and uses her humorous antics to win us over every time.

AMANA

A confirmation; truth; to be faithful.

Amana is the second middle child and still views herself as the baby of The Friendlettes. She is our touchy-feely daughter. She constantly seeks affirmation through hugs, kisses, and more. We call her our "cuddle-bug" because she is always looking for a lap to climb into and steal all the hugs and kisses she can get.

Though she is the smallest of the oldest three, she is definitely the fireball. Her feistiness allows her to hold her own in almost every situation. She is the strongest of the smaller three girls and doesn't mind picking any of them up to transport them to a different place in the house. Though her preference is to be in harmony with her sisters by loving and hugging them, when tested, she definitely holds her own!

Though Amana was very cautious of people early on, we have watched her little personality evolve to the point where she quickly embraces people and allows them into her little world. She still expects and demands undivided love and attention. She loves extremely hard, which has its ups and downs.

Lastly, Amana keeps our home grounded in love. She won't let a day go by without us showing her affection. Those who have received access into her little-big heart would say the same. She is our little pint of overflowing love.

LAYEL

Belonging to God; by God; devoted to God.

The last Friendlette takes on the true personality of a baby child. Layel is the comedienne. She finds a way to make others laugh about any given situation -- even if they don't want to. Her humor is unparalleled within our home. She creates little catch phrases and repeats them until she elicits the response she desires.

She completely milks the role of "the baby." She conducts herself as a thriving "threenager" until it is time for cleanup or bedtime. She masterfully wiggles her way out of chores and other responsibilities she deems too challenging and forfeits them to her gullible and loving older sisters.

At her age, Layel is probably the smartest of the four girls because she has marvelous examples to look to for help and assistance. Her inquisitive nature keeps her repertoire of words constantly growing. She loves and thrives on learning opportunities and soaks in the smallest action or activity she watches her sisters do.

1

Deal with It

MORNING MEDITATION

Psalm 84:11-12, New International Version

For the LORD God is a sun and shield; the LORD bestows favor and honor; no good thing does he withhold from those whose walk is blameless. LORD Almighty, blessed is the one who trusts in you.

EVENING DEVOTION

Psalm 37:23-24, New International Version

The LORD makes firm the steps of the one who delights in him; though he may stumble, he will not fall, for the LORD upholds him with his hand.

I wanted a son. Let's be honest, I do not think there is one man in the world who does not pray for a son to be born into his family to carry on his name and legacy. As you read through this devotional, it may seem as if I had mapped out a plan to be dominated by estrogen, Barbie dolls, and hair bows, but that was not at all the case.

I can remember each ultrasound as if it were yesterday. I remember hoping that the outcome of number "lines" would affirm my hopes for a son. Each time without fail, the outcome was the same–girls, girls, girls. I even remember going through the follow-up ultrasounds, praying that something had changed between visits. Still, the outcome was the same. One time, my hopes that all the doctors were wrong persisted until we were in the delivery room, hoping the bundle of joy's gender would surprise us all. Nevertheless, I had daughters four times in a row.

Now, as I watch the girls grow, I am daily amazed and honored that God chose me to handle such a great responsibility. Was this what I envisioned or desired? Not by any stretch of the imagination. However, it was the life God chose for me. Therefore, I chose to accept it with joy and embrace everything that came with raising four daughters in this ever-changing world.

Life in this new reality became easier when I made a decision after Londyn's birth. There are families who wish they could bring one child into the world and God had already blessed me with two. I decided that whatever the future held, I was going to live in that moment and trust the will of the Father to guide everything that would come from our lives.

As I continue to put everything in perspective, I thank God for the lot He dealt me. I often consider the fact that even with four successful pregnancies, we still lost two children in the process. Through each birth and miscarriage, the hand of God guided, graced, and carried us. The hand we were dealt may not have been the one we wanted, but it was the one God orchestrated. God made every situation we've faced work for our good.

As you examine your current situation in life, you may begin to look at your circumstances and wish that things could have been different. You may wish you were born into a different family, that you had a different environment growing up, that your parents were more active in your life, that you had made better choices–the list goes on. We must understand that at the end of the day, it does not matter what hand life has dealt you. What matters is that you serve the God of great grace Who has the ability to bring purpose out of every situation life brings your way.

Life does not always give us what we want. That's why our strength must always come from knowing that we serve the Giver of Life. He has the ability to take the worst circumstances and make them work out for our best. He doesn't need us to feel that every card is in the right place. He owns the deck! Regardless of what we may think or deal with, God knows how to navigate us through life.

Paul offers us powerful words of confirmation as it pertains to being settled in right where we are. *"I am not saying this because I am in need, for I have learned to be content whatever the circumstances." (Philippians 4:11)* One of the most powerful principles we could ever embrace centers on our ability to simply trust God and be content with whatever He has allowed towards our lives. Contentment is not a motion towards passivity in our actions; rather, it is a beckoning for those of us who truly trust God to not become shallow in our pursuit of Him when circumstances seem unfavorable towards us.

There is an even greater consolation to consider as we continue to walk God's path for our lives. That consolation is this: It could always be worse. Your situation may seem as if it is extremely challenging to your faith and focus, but with the proper perspective, you can realize that things could have been more challenging. Take your strength from a great man of faith named Job. Even when it seems as if life is working against you, maintain your resolve to worship God.

I stopped praying for a son after Layel was born. I realized that God put a grace on me to raise daughters. Instead of having a son, I would raise four women who understand what a true man and father look like in the lives of his daughters. I would have the privilege of being an example to young women in how to have open and honest communication with a father while knowing that his love would supersede any wrong that may occur. Today, I am honored in knowing that one day (waaaaaaay down the line), I would have helped to shape four young women for the glory of God and give them away to a man who loves God more than he loves them.

That is the hand I have been dealt. I own it. I embrace it. It is part of my purpose. I accept the challenge and look forward to fulfilling it completely. Look at your circumstances through the same lens. God is using your life to fulfill His purpose. Today, look at the hand you were dealt and prepare to fulfill all that God has entrusted to you.

PURPOSE PRAYER

Father,

The hand life dealt me may not have been what I wanted, but I trust You. I believe that You are going to use every situation for my good and Your glory. I know that You do not need my permission to work in and through me. I am privileged to see my life and the hand dealt to me through the eyes of faith. I put my trust in You.

I declare that life will not beat me, but instead, I can and will do all things through Christ Who gives me strength. I declare that adversity is an opportunity for my faith to grow. I declare that my best days are before me and that I will maximize every opportunity to show Your glory through my life. I declare that I am more than a conqueror in all things through You!

In Jesus' Name, Amen.

PURPOSE FOCUS

How much would your life be transformed if you focused on the blessings that God gave you versus the deficiencies you felt existed?

Today, how can you work towards overcoming your challenges and turning them into opportunities for success?

What problems have you been battling that may really be your blessing in disguise?

The Open Door

2

MORNING MEDITATION

Matthew 7:7-11, New Revised Standard Version

Ask, and it will be given you; search, and you will find; knock, and the door will be opened for you. For everyone who asks receives, and everyone who searches finds, and for everyone who knocks, the door will be opened. Is there anyone among you who, if your child asks for bread, will give a stone? Or if the child asks for a fish, will give a snake? If you then, who are evil, know how to give good gifts to your children, how much more will your Father in heaven give good things to those who ask him!

EVENING DEVOTION

Psalm 27:11-14, New Revised Standard Version

Teach me your way, O Lord, and lead me on a level path because of my enemies. Do not give me up to the will of my adversaries, for false witnesses have risen against me and they are breathing out violence. I believe that I shall see the goodness of the Lord in the land of the living. Wait for the Lord; be strong, and let your heart take courage; wait for the Lord!

Londyn, my second daughter, hates closed doors. She hates them with a passion. She hates them so much that there is no such thing as privacy in our home. If I want to take a nap behind closed doors, it's almost a guarantee that before my head hits the pillow, she will be knocking on the door trying to get in. I could tolerate it if she only knocked, but she doesn't stop there. If there is no answer, the situation escalates. The knocking turns into an outright beat down until someone finally answers. As soon as the door opens, she gives a broad, innocent smile and promptly throws her arms in the air to be picked up.

I decided to do a little experiment to gauge Londyn's reaction to closed doors. I went into the bathroom and stood behind the door. Within two minutes, she had commenced her knocking process. I went into the kitchen pantry that will only fit one person because of the shelf space. Same reaction. I even hid in the linen closet! Every door she knew I was behind produced the same reaction. Then I changed things up a bit. I closed the bathroom door and stood beside her in front of the door. She looked at the door, looked at me, lost interest, and subsequently waddled away to find something new to occupy her time. My experiment proved my thoughts exactly. It wasn't the door she was after–it was the person on the other side of it.

I am convinced that many of us miss opportunities hidden behind locked doors due to our lack of persistence. Grasp the open door principle: Never give up on a door when you know God is on the other side of it! We must be sure to not give up patience and persistence regarding God's plans for us. There are times He will test us to see how badly we want His will to become a reality in our lives. We must exhibit both patience and persistence in order for it to come to pass. The path to purpose is filled with doors that require persistent knocking in order for us to pass into the next phase of our lives.

The concept of patience and persistence goes against the grain of our modern "microwave society." We are conditioned to expect things quickly. Everything is so readily accessible to us! If we want to know our account balance, there's an app for that. Want to know the sports scores? There's an app for that. Need social media at your fingertips? There are apps for that. We want everything to be quick and easy, yet God's way requires pressing through prayer and practicing patience in order to obtain the promises on the other side of His divine door. It is easy to lose interest and persistence when God doesn't answer when we think He should. However, when we get persistent in our asking, seeking, and knocking, we will realize that the things truly breathed and inspired by God are worth the wait.

More often than not, God's greatest revelations are obtained through patience. Silence is not the consent to move forward, but rather a confirmation to be still and await direction. You may have to cry while you wait, but keep waiting. It may seem that life is passing you by, but understand that if this is the door God has ordained for your life, it will open at the right time. If you have asked of God, you will receive from Him. If you seek God, you will find Him. If you knock at God's door, He will open and reveal. Silence does not always equate to a "no." Will you keep knocking until God opens?

With each open door comes new opportunities and new adversaries. I Corinthians 16:9 reminds us that, *"...a great door for effective work has opened to me, and there are many who oppose me."* The most valuable principle of the open door can never revolve around the adversity that may accompany it, but on the sovereignty of the God who opened it in your favor. You have to trust the God who goes before you, makes your paths straight, and grants favorable opportunities for you to establish His Kingdom on the earth.

There will never be a door God will not open if it is in His will for your life. Today, refuse to allow impatience to override your persistence. Don't give up because the door has not yet been answered. Knock louder. What God has designed for you is for you. While you wait for the door to open, learn the power of patience and watch the will of God be revealed in your life!

PURPOSE PRAYER

Father,

I believe my greatest opportunities are behind the doors You have designed for my life. My focus is not on how big the door is, but on Your timing for the opening of each door in the right season of my life. Today, I embrace Your wisdom knowing that Your timing is perfect. While I wait for You to open the next door of opportunity, I will continue knocking in faith-filled persistence. In Your perfect timing, every door revealing a piece of my purpose will fly open at the appointed time.

I declare that Your will leads me to every door that needs to be opened in my life. I declare that I will be faithful to wait on Your timing while passionately pursuing who You created me to be. I declare that I will not get stuck in the stigma of wanting everything now, but that I will be patient throughout the process and trust You to open every door connected to my purpose.

In Jesus' Name, Amen.

PURPOSE FOCUS

When was the last time you remember God opening a door for you? How did you manage the opportunity?

What have you been praying for God to do for you, but felt like His voice went silent? Have you stopped knocking at your own advice or His direction?

If God were to open the door you have been praying the most about today, how would you manage that opportunity?

3

Making Adjustments

MORNING MEDITATION

Ecclesiastes 3:1-5, New Revised Standard Version

For everything there is a season, and a time for every matter under heaven: a time to be born, and a time to die; a time to plant, and a time to pluck up what is planted; a time to kill, and a time to heal; a time to break down, and a time to build up; a time to weep, and a time to laugh; a time to mourn, and a time to dance; a time to throw away stones, and a time to gather stones together; a time to embrace, and a time to refrain from embracing.

EVENING DEVOTION

Hebrews 13:6-9, New Revised Standard Version

So we can say with confidence, "The Lord is my helper; I will not be afraid. What can anyone do to me?" Remember your leaders, those who spoke the word of God to you; consider the outcome of their way of life, and imitate their faith. Jesus Christ is the same yesterday and today and forever.

The addition of Layel made it mandatory for another child to begin school. Londyn was next in line. Our prayer was that her transition from home to school would be a smooth one. Though Phineka had done an excellent job homeschooling the little ones in preparation for kindergarten, the attention the baby required coupled with Londyn's need for social development made it the perfect opportunity for her to begin school.

The first day of preschool was met with tears and tantrums. Though Londyn had spoken positively about wanting to start school, she had a change of heart on her first day. Instead of going into the school, she held on to the car door until I had to literally pry her away from it. When she met her teacher, she gripped my pants with all the strength in her little body and begged me not to leave. Walking away in that moment was one of the hardest things I have ever had to do.

During the first week, we saw no real improvement. When I picked her up after school, Londyn's eyes were accompanied by bags from the tears she had cried throughout her three-hour school day. As I contemplated the possibility of withdrawing Londyn and waiting to re-enroll her the next year, her teacher made a pivotal statement: "Give her two weeks. She just needs to adjust to this new change in her life."

By the third week of school, Londyn did not even want me to walk her to the door. She was waking up before us wanting to get to school as quickly as possible. When I walked her to class, she gave me a quick hug and kiss, rushed to her desk, and began her work. She was excited about homework and fell in love with her teacher. Little did I know, she had plans for a boyfriend. All of this happened simply because she adjusted to the changes that came into her life.

Fulfilling purpose in life is all about making changes and transitions. Anything that is not changing is probably dying. Whether we believe it or not, adjustments are necessary to fulfill God's plan for our lives. If we get stuck in the same patterns, same ways of thinking, and same routines, we subconsciously program God into our little box of ordinary. We serve a God Who wants to pour extraordinary into our lives! We have to be willing to make adjustments and transitions as necessary to become all that God has called us to be. Jesus Christ is the same yesterday, today, and forevermore (Hebrews 13:8). He is consistent in desiring the best for us. Yet, this does not mean that God is stuck in a routine; He simply desires to see our purpose fulfilled in the earth.

Transitions may start with tears, but they always end in triumph. When we are forced to adapt to new environments and new opportunities, it can be challenging at first. Not knowing what's next, why you are doing what you are doing, or how God is working behind the scenes often makes us anxious to understand what is transpiring in our lives. When we submit to the necessary adjustments, we will be able to look back and see that God was working everything in our favor all along.

Do not become so distracted by adjustments that you miss God's purpose being revealed in your life. Make no mistake about it–everything God allows you to experience is for His glory and your good. When we keep our focus on God throughout life's adjustments, we will see sooner rather than later how He is making His will a reality in our lives.

There is no single formula to figuring out God. It does not matter how long you have lived; God can change His method and methodology without consulting your will for approval. The truth of life is very simple: Those who are flexible will never be broken by life's shifts. I do not know when your change will come, but your ability to adapt to God's rhythm and pattern will be the greatest blessing your life could ever receive.

Life will force you to adjust, but God's Will becomes a reality when you submit to the change. Adjustments are not meant to be comfortable, but rather to stretch our faith and enable us to pursue our purpose in God. Today, ask God to reveal His hand in the midst of your transitions in life. When you see Him moving on your behalf, you can trust the adjustments you are thrust into. When you cannot see His hand, you can trust Him to navigate you through all life's circumstances. Purpose is revealed when you adjust to God's Will for your life!

PURPOSE PRAYER

Father,

My life has seen so many seasons of adjustment. Some of them I have accepted; others I fought against. Through it all, I trust You to lead me down the path You have purposed for my life so that my destiny will be revealed. I do not have to see and understand it all as long as I know that You are working in me and for me.

I declare that I will not be so rigid that I cannot synchronize my will to Yours. I declare that all stagnation and complacency in my life are broken off. I declare that I am submitted to You and that You will reveal Your purpose in everything I go through. I declare that even when I do not see it completely, I will trust You to guide me through every adjustment life presents!

In Jesus' Name, Amen.

PURPOSE FOCUS

How well do you manage change? When was the last time God forced you into an adjustment you were unprepared for?

Do you find it challenging to adapt to the unexpected?

How have you learned to trust God is seasons like that? Did it prove fruitful and beneficial?

The "Bandache"

4

MORNING MEDITATION

Psalm 147:1-6, New Revised Standard Version

Praise the Lord! How good it is to sing praises to our God; for he is gracious, and a song of praise is fitting. The Lord builds up Jerusalem; he gathers the outcasts of Israel. He heals the brokenhearted, and binds up their wounds. He determines the number of the stars; he gives to all of them their names. Great is our Lord, and abundant in power; his understanding is beyond measure. The Lord lifts up the downtrodden; he casts the wicked to the ground.

EVENING DEVOTION

II Corinthians 3:1-3, New Revised Standard Version

Are we beginning to commend ourselves again? Surely we do not need, as some do, letters of recommendation to you or from you, do we? You yourselves are our letter, written on our hearts, to be known and read by all; and you show that you are a letter of Christ, prepared by us, written not with ink but with the Spirit of the living God, not on tablets of stone but on tablets of human hearts.

Contrary to popular belief, I have discovered that girls are rough. Sure, Phineka does a tremendous job getting the girls all cute and dolled up, but don't let the matching clothes and cute smiles fool you—our girls can be just as rough (if not rougher) than boys. Sometimes they wrestle for play and other times they are literally at each other's throats. Phineka and I are pretty sure we only catch about fifty percent of their sisterly violence which is why we missed the situation we eventually came to refer to as "The Cover-Up."

It was a warm, autumn afternoon and the girls were outside playing as they typically do. All of the sudden, there was a shriek that could be heard in the highest heavens followed by the pitter-patter of little feet racing through the screen door to try and explain what happened. As the girls presented themselves, we discovered that the tears belonged to Amana. She tried her best to explain what happened, but between her outrageous tears and lack of vocabulary, all that came out was, "I hurt!" Ashriel blamed it on Londyn. Londyn pointed to Amana. Amana pointed back at both of them. To this day, we're still not sure what happened.

What was even more amazing about this scuffle was the cut on Amana's arm. Maybe "cut" isn't the right word. There was a scratch stretching about one-quarter of a centimeter on her arm that barely shed any blood. As I began to survey the damage done, she repeatedly told me she needed a "bandache." After playing doctor and satisfactorily covering the scratch, the girls went along their merry way.

Two months later, there was a barely noticeable mark left on Amana's arm where the injury occurred. However, Amana still cried out for a "bandache" every day. The scratch was completely healed, but something made her think she still needed to keep it covered. There was no more bleeding or pain, yet she still desired to cover up what had already been healed.

Does this remind you of anything in your life? Have you ever found yourself trying to cover up areas that God has already healed just to be sure you would never be hurt again? Is there something God has delivered you from that you still refuse to uncover? What I love about our awesome God is that He never allows us to go through an experience without the expressed intent of teaching us something. The lesson may be small, but it is still valuable. Even when our hurts are self-imposed, God will use them to make us better. You never know how valuable your experience could be in the life of someone else until you are willing to expose it.

This may be one of the more challenging devotionals, but it serves as a reminder of two things. First, God is the Healer of all things. He heals us physically, touches us spiritually, repairs us emotionally--the list could go on for the length of eternity. The truth of the matter is, God does heal. It does not matter how shattered or broken it has been. Nor does it matter how deep the wound goes. From the shallowest of abrasions to the deepest of soul wounds, God is a Healer.

Second, God heals us to heal others. Your experience is never just for you. It's for you to help someone else in their process. Think about it. Christ's experience at Calvary was not just for Him. It was done for you, me, and all humanity. It was one incident that affected all people. Your story may not have the same reach as Jesus' crucifixion and resurrection, but it is still meant to be shared. The power of your testimony is that it no longer needs to be covered. You are healed and now you can help heal others by the word of your testimony. Do not cover up what God has called you to proclaim.

How can we be so sure that God heals? It's simple. In Psalm 147, David said the Lord heals the brokenhearted and, in short, nurses every one of our wounds to full recovery. If you have ever broken a limb or know someone who has, you know that the cast the doctor places on the broken area is only temporary. Its purpose is to reset the bone and allow it to heal properly. When the time is right, the cast is removed and the limb is restored to its original state. In the same way, God uses our painful situations as an opportunity to set us back on the right path. When our hearts are open to the Holy Spirit, He is able to heal us like no other and enable us to realign ourselves with His vision and plan for our lives. Life's situations may break our hearts, but they don't have to remain broken. God wants to heal you completely.

This is your day to take off the "bandache". When you do, you'll find that what you thought was helping you heal was really covering up what God had already healed. Don't allow the experiences of your past to haunt or intimidate you from moving forward in your purpose. This is your day to get up and go in the direction God has designed for your life.

PURPOSE PRAYER

Father,

My life and heart have been broken, but I believe that You are a Healer. In fact, I have felt Your healing power over my life many times before. Today, I choose to walk in total healing so that I can fulfill Your purpose for me.

I declare that I will not make another excuse to cover up what I have been delivered from. I declare that I am healed spiritually, emotionally, mentally, and physically. I declare that my life is an open book read by all people so they can learn that God still heals and delivers. I declare no more cover-ups! The Band-Aids are removed and I receive the full restoration only found in You.

In Jesus' Name, Amen.

PURPOSE FOCUS

What is the most painful experience you have endured? When did you turn it over to God to remedy what you could not manage?

Have you ever self-sabotaged your own healing process by refusing to let people in? What did/would it take for you to let your guard down?

Do you trust people to know your pain and not leave you alone? Explain.

Praying God's Will

5

MORNING MEDITATION

James 1:5-8, New Revised Standard Version

If any of you is lacking in wisdom, ask God, who gives to all generously and ungrudgingly, and it will be given you. But ask in faith, never doubting, for the one who doubts is like a wave of the sea, driven and tossed by the wind; for the doubter, being double-minded and unstable in every way, must not expect to receive anything from the Lord.

EVENING DEVOTION

Matthew 6:5-6, New Revised Standard Version

And whenever you pray, do not be like the hypocrites; for they love to stand and pray in the synagogues and at the street corners, so that they may be seen by others. Truly I tell you, they have received their reward. But whenever you pray, go into your room and shut the door and pray to your Father who is in secret; and your Father who sees in secret will reward you.

I will never forget Phineka's pregnancy with Londyn. It had to be one of the most dramatic experiences of our lives. I was finishing up my final year of graduate school at Oral Roberts University and working full-time on staff at Greenwood Christian Center (now Transformation Church). Just a few months prior to this pregnancy, Phineka had a miscarriage. Needless to say, we were all at a heightened awareness as we embraced the opportunity to bring another life into the world.

At this time, Ashriel had started to operate in the gifts of the Spirit. She would pray for anyone and anything in a heartbeat. If you had a headache, she was laying hands on you and praying. She would tell you what she felt like God was saying to her for your life. Our home and church life was very interesting because of our little prayer warrior.

Every night, Ashriel made it her business to lay hands on Phineka's stomach and pray for a brother. She was determined to be the only girl and her heart longed for a boy in the home almost as much as mine did. Every night as we prayed together, she would thank God for her new baby brother. Her heart was set, her prayers were consistent, and she was faithful to what she wanted God to do for her family.

I will never forget the car ride to the ultrasound to discover the baby's gender. As we drove down the road, I noticed Ashriel sitting in her car seat with her arms folded and an angry expression on her face. I asked her what was wrong and her response was stern and to-the-point: "I'm mad at God!" Her words begged more questions, so Phineka asked her why and her next response was simply: "I prayed for a brother, and God is giving me a sister. God didn't give me what I wanted!"

Phineka and I did not know if we should be more shocked at Ashriel's anger with God or her supposed prophecy. Sure enough, her words were true. When we realized that it was little Londyn and not a boy growing in Phineka's belly, Ashriel responded matter-of-factly, "See, I told you! That's why I'm mad at God!" Though it took a couple of months for her to recover from the setback of her prayers falling short, she learned a valuable lesson early on in life.

So often, we miss God's Plan because we do not pray His Will. It happens so easily. We know what we want, how we want it, and when we want it, all without truly considering what God's Will is. We pray "good" prayers without considering if they are in alignment with God's Plan for our lives. Good words outside of God's Will do not produce fruit in our lives. It is not enough to pray "good" prayers. We must be committed to praying God's Will.

There has to be a clear distinction between praying what you want and praying God's will. This does not mean that God does not want to bless us with our desires. However, beyond fulfilling our personal desires, God wants to see His perfect will manifest in our lives. When our prayers do not align with His Purpose, we end up praying amiss and falling short of His Will. Our wants should never supersede God's Will. When God's Will becomes real in our heart, our prayers will align with His.

We can never become so concerned with what we want that we miss what He wills. Please do not mistake me–God wants to bless you with everything you need to fulfill His Purpose for your life. He wants to blow your mind with His ability to bless you beyond your wildest imaginations. We must understand that His Blessings can never become more of a motivation than seeing His Will become real in our lives. What He blesses us with is simply a benefit of our freedom to walk in His Purpose for our lives. There is nothing wrong with having stuff, but there is great error in stuff having us.

Trust God to come into your heart and alter your prayer life today. Even if you have been praying His Will for your life, let this be the day that God reveals His Heart and Nature to you. Let this be the day you embrace the total reality of Who He created you to be. Do not allow another day to pass with you merely praying your will–let God's Will dominate everything you do!

PURPOSE PRAYER

Father,

I know that in my past I have been guilty of praying my will and not Yours. Right now, I desire to pray only Your Will for every aspect of my life. I do not want my desires to lead me astray. My purpose is great and I do not want to frustrate Your Grace by only wanting my way. Today, I want to see Your Will made even more of a reality in my life.

I declare that my will is in complete submission to Your Will for my life. I declare that I will not pray amiss or in error, but that Your Desires will reign in my heart and life. I declare that what I pray in secret is in alignment with Your Desires and that it will become a reality in my life. I declare that my purpose is found in the center of Your Will and I am seeking it like never before!

In Jesus' Name, Amen.

PURPOSE FOCUS

Have you recovered from the last time God told you no?

What would you say is the most challenging thing about wholeheartedly submitting to God's will?

How has experience and wisdom taught you not to kick against the masterpiece God was making through His will in your story?

Learning God's Voice

6

MORNING MEDITATION

John 10:1-5, New International Version

Most assuredly, I say to you, he who does not enter the sheepfold by the door, but climbs up some other way, the same is a thief and a robber. But he who enters by the door is the shepherd of the sheep. To him the doorkeeper opens, and the sheep hear his voice; and he calls his own sheep by name and leads them out. And when he brings out his own sheep, he goes before them; and the sheep follow him, for they know his voice. Yet they will by no means follow a stranger, but will flee from him, for they do not know the voice of strangers.

EVENING DEVOTION

Psalm 50:1-6, New International Version

The Mighty One, God, the Lord, speaks and summons the earth from the rising of the sun to where it sets. From Zion, perfect in beauty, God shines forth. Our God comes and will not be silent; a fire devours before him, and around him a tempest rages. He summons the heavens above and the earth, that he may judge his people: "Gather to me this consecrated people, who made a covenant with me by sacrifice." And the heavens proclaim his righteousness, for he is a God of justice.

It is always interesting when I leave town. When we moved to Arizona a couple of years ago, my daughters grew accustomed to having me at home. When I do leave, they go through intense, dramatic withdrawal.

What I have learned through this experience is that my girls have learned my voice. They know when I am excited and happy to speak with them. They also know when I am displeased by things that have transpired in my absence. Their sensitivity to my voice has grown as they have grown familiar with me.

On a recent trip, Phineka told me the girls were having a tough time getting along. Instead of scolding them herself, she wanted me to talk with them to see if they would straighten up. As she handed the phone to Ashriel, I could hear the trembling of her voice as she attempted to decipher the tone of my voice. The moment she recognized my unhappy tone, the floodgates of teary emotions were loosed. Ashriel's desire was to please her parents and the voice that she heard was one that, although never raised, let her know Daddy was serious.

As we grow in our relationship with God, our sensitivity to His voice, direction, and plan should also grow. The closer we walk with Him, the more we should be able to distinguish submission to His will from pursuing our own. Learning God's voice means we are attempting to learn His plan for our lives. The more we familiarize ourselves with Him, the closer we come to staying on His path for our lives.

There are many voices attempting to influence our direction in life. There is the voice of our inner circle that tries to direct us based on their desires or doubts. There is the voice of the naysayers who do not believe in anything we do or the purpose for which we were created. There is even the voice of the wishy-washy who one moment are, "yes men" and the next, change their opinions. At the end of the day, we must resolve that the voice of God is the only voice we must depend on to release purpose into our lives. You can still respect the opinions of others while wholeheartedly seeking the voice and confirmation of the Father.

In John 10, Jesus taught that there is a major difference between those who understand the voice and direction of God and those who do not. The simple difference is this: Those who understand God's voice have a relationship; those who do not have a religion. Religion robs us of the relationship Jesus so desires to have with us through His Holy Spirit. Religion avoids the Way and instead, attempts to climb in by another way, denying us the opportunity to hear God's voice. Religion is not pure religion according to James 1:27, but rather the conglomeration of routines, works, and traditions that do not stem from a sincere desire to know or serve God.

So how do you learn the voice of God? For starters, fully let Him into your heart. Second, remove every hindrance that attempts to separate you from Him and remain open to His instruction. Third, invest time in your relationship. The same way you invest in your other relationships is the same consideration, time, and devotion you should give to God.

Finally, as much as you talk to Him, stop and listen. God speaks to us through His Word, through the inner leading of the Holy Spirit, and yes, at times through an audible voice. In fact, He will even send others into our lives as His representatives to speak on His behalf. As you invest time cultivating your relationship with God, you will gain sensitivity to Him in every area of your life. As you open your heart to God, you will begin to hear and understand His voice like never before! You cannot fulfill His purpose for your life without being familiar to His call and His voice. Listen to Him!

PURPOSE PRAYER

Father,

I need Your direction in every area of my life. I want to hear Your voice like never before. I trust You, the Shepherd of my life, to lead me in the direction that is best. Help me to not wander like a sheep and test your grace. I want to know You, follow You, and wholly submit my life to Your will. Help me to not only hear, but listen to Your voice.

I declare that my spiritual ears are sensitive to Your voice. I declare that as I submit to Your purpose, my plans are synchronized with Yours. I declare that as I listen for Your voice, You will guide my steps and Your desires will manifest in my life. I declare that my ears are open, my heart is free, and my spirit is willing to follow wherever You lead.

In Jesus' Name, Amen.

PURPOSE FOCUS

Have you ever been challenged in deciphering God's voice over that of your own? How did you come to the correct conclusion?

How sensitive have your ears become to knowing God's voice?

Once you know what His voice sounds like, do you still have trouble blocking out the voice of others? Why or why not?

7

Do We Really Need All This?

MORNING MEDITATION

Matthew 11:29-30, New International Version

Come to me, all you who are weary and burdened, and I will give you rest. Take my yoke upon you and learn from me, for I am gentle and humble in heart, and you will find rest for your souls. For my yoke is easy and my burden is light.

EVENING DEVOTION

I Peter 5:6-7, New International Version

Humble yourselves, therefore, under God's mighty hand, that he may lift you up in due time. Cast all your anxiety on him because he cares for you.

Since we've been married, Phineka and I have lived in our home state of Alabama for less than three months. Between school and ministry opportunities, we have been as close as two hours and as far as two days from Alabama. This is why, just as in one of the other devotionals, travel is always an interesting challenge for our family. The luggage alone is enough to make us want to reconsider traveling!

On a recent trip to visit our parents, we arrived at the airport and parked. We pulled out the double-stroller, three large pieces of luggage, four carry-on bags, and a pacifier (we never left home without one). After Ashriel and I ran the luggage to the check-in, Phineka took the stroller, all of the remaining girls, and two carry-on pieces to the gate while I parked the car. After parking and making it through security, I was greeted by faces that looked exhausted (with the exception of Londyn and Amana who had been rolling around in the stroller in pure comfort and amusement). Then, as if she'd had a sudden epiphany, Ashriel looked around at everything we'd brought with us and asked, "Mommy, Daddy, do we really need all this?"

We boarded the plane in laughter and reflection. We honestly over-packed. Phineka has a tendency to pack for an additional two weeks beyond the actual length of our stay. Sometimes, I think it's in hopes that we'll move back home. Other times, I think it's a mother's intuition to make sure everyone has more than enough clothes for the trip. Nevertheless, we could have stood to leave some stuff at home. We wouldn't even get a chance to wear some of the outfits on this particular trip. We were accustomed to having so much with us, but there wasn't a need for it all. I mean, will a two-year-old really wear seventeen outfits on a ten-day trip? In the end, our tons of extra baggage became more of a burden than a blessing.

In life, we tend to carry around unnecessary baggage. We have a myriad of reasons for holding on to it when in all actuality, we know that it should have been released many years ago. There's a place of comfort we often build around ourselves that gives us a false sense of protection. The danger, however, is that carrying the wrong things for too long can cause us to miss the opportunity to pick up what really is necessary for the next phase of our lives.

It isn't a coincidence that Jesus taught us to cast our cares, concerns, and baggage on Him. Why? Because left in our own hands, most of our baggage turns to bitterness. When the root of bitterness is present in our lives, the possibility of truly fulfilling everything God has called us to be and do is greatly reduced. We find excuses to justify holding on to the "stuff" we know we should let go of. If we took an honest assessment of our lives, we would probably find that we are not holding the stuff–the stuff is holding us!

What burdens are you carrying that have become more of a hindrance than a help in fulfilling the purpose of God for your life? How many times have you told yourself you can't get over something because you simply refuse to try? What baggage have you packed that has been weighing you down and keeping you grounded by the mishaps of the past? Whatever it may be, the question for you is simply: Do you really need all this stuff?

What have you made accommodations for in your life that are illegitimate and could be removed? For our trip, I'm sure that just removing one or two outfits per person would have made all the difference. What can you remove from your life that isn't necessary? The weight of extra baggage is too heavy for you to carry because you weren't designed to carry it alone. God will only intervene when you make the conscious confession that you don't really need everything you insist on carrying. Start unpacking your bags and decide only to carry the things that will help you fulfill God's call on your life. Leave some stuff behind!

PURPOSE PRAYER

Heavenly Father,

I refuse to allow the baggage of yesterday to hinder me from the future You have for me. It may prove challenging, but I resolve to begin unpacking and casting all of my cares upon You. And even when my emotions make it difficult to let go, I trust You to help me unload; I am not in this alone.

I declare that I will not allow my baggage to weigh me down. I declare that You are the Burden-Bearer. I declare that as You lift the baggage from my life that I will not succumb to the temptation of picking it back up. Today, I give it to You trusting that You will dispose of it so that I can focus solely on You. I refuse to carry unnecessary baggage in my life!

In Jesus' Name, Amen.

PURPOSE FOCUS

What have you been carrying around in life that you no longer need? When was the last time you intentionally "unpacked" that which was not necessary?

When was the last time you felt like your load was burdensome?

If you let everything go that was weighing you down today, how much differently do you believe your life would look?

8

I Need More Time

MORNING MEDITATION

James 4:7-8, New Revised Standard Version

Submit yourselves therefore to God. Resist the devil, and he will flee from you. Draw near to God, and he will draw near to you. Cleanse your hands, you sinners, and purify your hearts, you double-minded.

EVENING DEVOTION

James 4:13-17, New Revised Standard Version

Come now, you who say, "Today or tomorrow we will go to such and such a town and spend a year there, doing business and making money." Yet you do not even know what tomorrow will bring. What is your life? For you are a mist that appears for a little while and then vanishes. Instead you ought to say, "If the Lord wishes, we will live and do this or that." As it is, you boast in your arrogance; all such boasting is evil. Anyone, then, who knows the right thing to do and fails to do it, commits sin.

One of the most difficult things about being a husband, father, pastor, and traveling minister is time. Balance is undoubtedly the key. There is a delicacy in balancing a family that cannot take a backseat to everything else transpiring in my life. Though the external demands are often challenging, next to God, there is nothing more valuable to me than family.

On one of my trips, I Skyped home to talk to my wife and girls. As Londyn and Amana dominated the talk time, I noticed my Ashriel drifting off into the background with gloomy, saddened eyes. At first, I chalked it up to her normal I-want-Daddy-home-with-us pouting. However, as I continued to talk to the younger girls, I realized that there was something deeper going on.

After we had ended the Skype session, I called my wife and asked to speak to Ashriel. Once she got the phone, she took off for the bathroom, locked herself in, and sat in the bathtub to talk to her Daddy. As I began inquiring about her behavior, she quickly told me, "Daddy, I need more time! My sisters always hog the camera, and I don't ever get to talk. We don't get to go on daddy-daughter dates with just me and you anymore because of them. They took all of my time, and I need more time!"

As I listened to Ashriel, my heart was immediately convicted. She was right. With the newest additions to the family, the new lead pastor position, and everything that came along with both, my time and allegiance to Ashriel had become divided. Her plea was legitimate. She didn't ask for much; she just wanted her share of time with me. She was entitled to that. She deserved that. By right of being my child, it was a fundamental requirement.

As I mulled over her requests, I remembered how our Father God often makes the same plea to us. It is so easy for us to become encumbered by everything that transpires in our lives! Our jobs, families, commitments, and desires take the front seat, while we force God to take the backseat in our lives. Please, hear my heart: This doesn't mean that you love God any less. However, it's possible that He has become less of a priority in your life. You still love Him, but you feel the strain of the relationship. Through the words of my daughter, you can hear Him pleading with you saying, "I just want more time."

The cares of this world have a way of drowning out the call to a closer relationship with God. We will always be able to find excuses that keep us from cultivating our relationship with Him. Ashriel's plea reminded me of the time before I was a pastor, before there was a house full of children, and before life became so demanded. She reminded me of the time when I effortlessly made my time with her a priority. Though I wasn't consciously looking for an excuse to not spend time with her, my actions spoke volumes. From her perspective, everything else had become more important than her. If God were to speak to your heart right now, what do you think He would say about the time you spend with Him?

So often, we make vows to do better with our time in the future, when in actuality, today is the best day to spend time with God and correct the glaring errors of our time management. It may start out small, even as simple as going through this devotional each day. Yet, as opportunity allows, our relationship with God should grow stronger with each passing day. And as that relationship grows stronger, so does our realization of the power of God's purpose over our lives.

The truth of the matter is that we have time for what we consider a priority. Today, as you begin to make strides in your relationship with God, it is important to make Him your number one priority. Stop considering prayer, meditation, and study the last resort; make it your only option. As we move closer to God, His Word promises that He will move closer to us. As we move closer to God, we'll begin to notice that our attachments to things not like Him will begin to fade away. Our hands, which represent our actions, will become pure. Our hearts, which represent our attitudes, will become focused on the sole objective of pleasing God. Choose to make God first in your life today. As you keep Him first, everything else concerning your life will come into alignment with Him.

PURPOSE PRAYER

Heavenly Father,

My time is valuable because You gave it to me. Today, I promise to give You more of my time. Please forgive me for the times I've subconsciously devalued the need to invest time in our relationship. I choose to make You the top priority in my day. I seek You first and know that You will add everything else I need in life. Each day I am drawing closer to You.

I declare that You are first and foremost in my life and that I manage my time accordingly. I declare that as I make You my priority, everything else concerning my life will fall into place. I declare that our relationship grows and becomes all it should be for Your glory and that Your purpose is fulfilled in my life.

In Jesus' Name, Amen.

PURPOSE FOCUS

With what have your over-saturated your life? What is preventing you from spending time with God?

How could you better manage your time to ensure that you incorporate time for personal growth and development?

What have you made a priority that should probably only be an option at best?

9

The Search

MORNING MEDITATION

Psalm 63:1-5, New International Version

You, God, are my God, earnestly I seek you; I thirst for you, my whole being longs for you, in a dry and parched land where there is no water. I have seen you in the sanctuary and beheld your power and your glory. Because your love is better than life, my lips will glorify you. I will praise you as long as I live, and in your name I will lift up my hands. I will be fully satisfied as with the richest of foods; with singing lips my mouth will praise you.

EVENING DEVOTION

Jeremiah 29:12-13, New International Version

Then you will call on me and come and pray to me, and I will listen to you. You will seek me and find me when you seek me with all your heart.

With our three oldest daughters, the pacifier stage turned out to be one of the most critical junctures in our family. Ashriel kept a "binky" until she was almost three. Londyn held full-fledged conversations as hers hung between her lips. Amana's obsession, however, takes the cake. Her addiction to "pappies" sent us to the nearest store in the wee hours of the morning so she could be consoled by her "best friend."

One night Amana came into our room around two in the morning because she couldn't find her pappy. I sent her back to her room to look, but she couldn't find it. I convinced her to climb in bed with Phineka and me, but sleep would not come until she had a pacifier. Finally, out of desperation (and frustration), I put out an APB on all pacifiers in the house. I looked under beds, in closets, through cabinets, and even in the washer and dishwasher, but to no avail. After thirty minutes of searching, I went back and tried to convince her to sleep without one. That caused even more tears than the ones she'd already shed. Amana was determined that she would not sleep until her pacifier–any pacifier–was recovered.

In my final act of desperation, I decided to check our truck. There, nestled beside the buckle of Amana's car seat, was one lonely pappy. I quickly washed it off and placed it in her mouth, and within two minutes, she was fast asleep. Her desperation for satisfaction caused her to reject sleep until she got what she wanted. No matter who searched or how long it took, she knew what she needed and would not stop until she had it.

When I laid back down to sleep, the Holy Spirit spoke to me what has since become the heart of this devotion:

"How strongly are you searching for Me? Are you desperate enough to learn My will that you will turn on the lights to every dark place in your life until you uncover My desires? Will you search for Me until your soul is satisfied and you receive everything you need? Will your pursuit cause others to awaken from their slumber and begin their own search to know Me better? If you seek Me, you will find Me, but you must be willing to pursue Me."

Though we are all in various stages of our walk with God, we must continually be willing to pursue His will for our lives.

We must be resolute in our stance and refuse to accept anything less than His desires for us. The stronger your pursuit, the more fulfilling your life will be once you attain God's will. Searching for Him must be a daily experience. Our hunger and thirst for righteousness cannot be like a switch that we flip on and off at will, but rather something that transpires in spite of our feelings and personal pursuits. When you search for Him with your whole heart, there is a Bible-guarantee that you will find Him.

Your life will be consumed by what you pursue. As the Lord spoke through the Prophet Jeremiah to the Children of Israel about their time of exile, He made one thing certain: When you pray and return to Me with your whole heart, I will answer you. Their pursuit had lost its focus. They became enamored with the peoples surrounding them and the gods thereof. They pursued everything but God, and their search led them further and further away from the heart and will of God–spiritually and physically.

It is the same in our own lives. We cannot allow people and things to hinder our pursuit of God. No matter what may form our list of priorities, we can never let any of them supersede our constant search for God. We must daily seek His will for our lives as well as the lives of those connected to us. Take time to assess how you can renew your pursuit of God today. What has blocked you from it? What must be removed so you can give Him your whole heart? When we seek Him, we will find Him. It's guaranteed.

PURPOSE PRAYER

Heavenly Father,

Today I recognize that I have been complacent in my search for You. Teach me how to search for You with my whole heart. My desire is to never allow our relationship to become stagnant or stale. Refresh me this day with Your power, Your presence, and a renewed desire to pursue You.

I declare that from here on out, I will seek You with my whole heart. I declare that my heart longs for You and my soul thirsts for You until I am filled to overflowing. I declare that I need You more than I need anything else in this world My search will never be complete and my passion daily renewed as I seek You in every area of my life.

In Jesus' Name, Amen.

PURPOSE FOCUS

When was the last time you relentlessly pursued God? How did that time/season of your life benefit your personal purpose?

What has taken His place in your search/pursuit? When did this replacement happen?

How can you alter your heart from what you have placed above Him?

Who are You Imitating? 10

MORNING MEDITATION

Philippians 4:8-9, New Revised Standard Version

Finally, beloved, whatever is true, whatever is honorable, whatever is just, whatever is pure, whatever is pleasing, whatever is commendable, if there is any excellence and if there is anything worthy of praise, think about these things. Keep on doing the things that you have learned and received and heard and seen in me, and the God of peace will be with you.

EVENING DEVOTION

Ephesians 5:1-2, New Revised Standard Version

Therefore be imitators of God, as beloved children, and live in love, as Christ loved us and gave himself up for us, a fragrant offering and sacrifice to God.

Like all siblings, our children always find a way to drive each other crazy at whatever time they deem appropriate. In most cases, all times are appropriate. One of Londyn's favorite games to play was the human playback machine. She'd follow Ashriel all over the house doing whatever she did, saying whatever she said, and acting however she acted.

The game quickly became old. One afternoon, Ashriel became so frustrated with the "game" that she began yelling at Londyn.

"Why do you keep following me?! Why do you keep doing what I do and saying what I say?!"

Londyn gazed up at her sister with her big brown eyes and stated matter-of-factly, "Because you're my sister. I'm supposed to!"

Granted, we were not one hundred percent sure whether Londyn meant she was supposed to annoy Ashriel or be like her big sister, but it still provides us with tremendous insight.

Who does your life imitate? If people were to observe your walk, talk, dress, interactions, and overall lifestyle, would it scream "I belong to God?" Would it be apparent that your life is surrendered to God or would people see more of you than they see of Him? As we grow in our relationship with God, our desires must become aligned with His will for our lives. As we begin to give up our own selfish thoughts and ideas and embrace God's desires for us, it will become apparent to us as well as to others that we truly belong to God.

The Apostle Paul gave each of us a very strong word of instruction and encouragement. He told us to imitate God; to allow everything we do in word and deed to mimic the heart of the Father. In this world, it's so easy to get caught up in imitating something that we forget the simplicity of being ourselves. When we choose to imitate God in all we do, it takes the unspoken pressure out of every interaction. We don't rely on our own wisdom, but instead, we trust in the power of God's Word to shape our lives and give us the right words to speak in each situation. When we become true imitators of God, we remove the burden of being cheap imitations of anyone else.

Often in society, imitations are viewed as negative even though most of what we develop is a cheap imitation of someone else's idea. Paul reminds us that the best we can do in our growth in God is to become imitators of Him. What does that mean? To imitate Christ means to keep our spirit, mind, heart, and actions in alignment with His Word. This means that truth and honor are at the forefront of our mind. Justice and purity rule our hearts. Pleasing God and living commendably are the seeds of our transformation and the things that are excellent and worthy of praise are the fruit of our actions.

When God's truth becomes the ruling factor in our mind, it is easy for us to imitate the character of Christ. This kind of thought life suggests growth, progress, and maturity in our relationship with God. You will never be a cheap imitation as long as you imitate the real thing! Today, choose to begin imitating Christ in everything you do and watch the fruit of change transform your life!

PURPOSE PRAYER

Heavenly Father,

I want to be an imitator of You and You alone. Help me to abandon thinking that takes my focus off You. Today from here on out, I completely dedicate my heart, soul, and mind to You. Remove everything in my life that makes me a cheap imitation. Allow my life and love for You to point others to You!

I declare that my mind is focused on things that are good, trustworthy, honorable, pure, and just. I declare that my heart allows the free flow of every godly attribute. I declare that the world will never cause me to be deterred from Your will in any area of my life. You are the Head of my life. Thank You Lord for making me like You and empowering me to live a life that pleases You.

In Jesus' Name, Amen.

PURPOSE FOCUS

If a stranger were to watch your life for 24 hours, would they see the reflection of Christ in your life and actions? Why or why not?

Where do you find the greatest challenges in following the footsteps that He has ordered for your life?

What will it take for you to become comfortable in the purpose He created you for?

11

Keep Moving

MORNING MEDITATION

Philippians 3:12-14, New International Version

Not that I have already obtained all this, or have already arrived at my goal, but I press on to take hold of that for which Christ Jesus took hold of me. Brothers and sisters, I do not consider myself yet to have taken hold of it. But one thing I do: Forgetting what is behind and straining toward what is ahead, I press on toward the goal to win the prize for which God has called me heavenward in Christ Jesus.

EVENING DEVOTION

Isaiah 43:18-19, New International Version

Forget the former things; do not dwell on the past. See, I am doing a new thing! Now it springs up; do you not perceive it? I am making a way in the wilderness and streams in the wasteland.

Traveling is always an adventure, especially with young children. Be it by car, bus, train, or plane, you never know what to expect when little ones are onboard. Potty breaks, inability to sit still, altercations over someone's head being too close to the other's...need I say more? Oh, and I can't forget the looks of people on the plane once they realize you have small children. The eye rolls, heavy exhales, and silent prayers that you are not sitting by them are unforgettable! Every parent in America can breathe a huge sigh of relief–our struggle is real!

A while back, Phineka had to take her first of many trips alone with the girls. There was a death in the family, and I needed to stay behind and tie up some loose ends before I could fly out and join them the next day. As we sat in the airport, Phineka was five months pregnant and preparing to embark on the flight with the girls. I could tell that she was slightly overwhelmed. Heck, I would have backed out of the trip if I were her. I convinced her that it would be alright and that the girls would behave. Since it was a red-eye flight, everyone would be sound asleep, and they would get through Baggage Claim without incident. As I attempted to encourage her, something in the pit of my stomach told me that my little angels wouldn't live up to my lofty expectations.

I could see tears rolling down her face as I walked her to the gate. She promised me she was fine and that she'd make it through. As I stood from a short distance and watched them load the carry-on luggage for a security check, the show began. Amana was rolling on the floor and tossing her shoes about in complete disdain over the fact that airport security told her she could keep them on. Londyn then broke out into a full-fledged tantrum once she realized that I was no longer walking with them. Ashriel tried her best to console her mother and sisters as tears began rolling down her face as well. I wanted to morph into Superman and jump through the security gate, but I realized that jail was my kryptonite. As much as I love my family, I knew I couldn't cross the security line because I wasn't cut out for the Hard Times. Through it all, Phineka somehow managed to keep moving everyone forward.

Once on the plane, Phineka called me. "Bae, I'm ok. The girls didn't want to act right. I was crying, but I kept on moving. The stewardess helped me get the girls on board. I knew I needed to keep on moving and now we are on the plane. We are ok."

The key to her progress was to move forward despite the various obstacles that came her way. She refused to stop moving.

There are times in all of our lives when it seems as if the obstacles blocking the road to our destiny far outweigh our desire to progress. We have all encountered moments and seasons when it seemed as if moving backward was better than being stagnant or even attempting to move forward. In those challenges, our eyes must remain fixed on the prize that is set before us. We must remain focused on the task at hand and simultaneously keep our confidence in God. Our confidence can never be in our own ability. It is only the ability of God that will give us exactly what we need when we need it.

If Phineka would have allowed the temper-tantrums and shoe tossing to stop her from moving forward, she would have never known that help was waiting for her on the other side. If her focus had been on the disheartening happenings of the moment, she would have jeopardized what we had already invested in the flights. God will always send the right people into your life at the right time to help you navigate your greatest challenges. God knows what you can handle. Furthermore, He knows when it is time to send you the help you need to push you forward. Never doubt the timing of

God. He always knows what you need at the exact moment you need it. His timing is impeccable!

The Apostle Paul reminds us that going forward requires us to focus on that which is ahead and not behind. You can never get to your destination if you are constantly focused on where you are not. In short, your attitude, mentality, and perspective have to shift forward so you won't sit back and allow life to pass you. You may not be everything you desire to be today, but you certainly are not who you were yesterday. Forget the things behind you because as you keep moving forward, a new thing is about to spring up in your life!

You may be in a season where you don't know up from down, but keep moving forward. It may seem as if the One who should be walking with you is watching from a distance, but never stop moving forward. Challenges come, storms arise, and difficulties may persist, but backward is not your answer. Move forward in your purpose and God's promise. Help is just over the horizon. Keep moving forward!

PURPOSE PRAYER

Heavenly Father,

My desire today is to continue moving forward in the purpose You have planned for my life. Though life's circumstances have a tendency to seem overwhelming, I am determined to see Your plan revealed in my life. This day, I choose to move forward.

I declare that every **obstacle** is simply an **opportunity** for me to refocus. I declare that every mountain is a milestone for me to remember Your faithfulness. I declare that in every circumstance, I will create a way to praise You. In all things, my focus, my attitude, and my direction are focused on the future!

In Jesus' Name, Amen.

PURPOSE FOCUS

What has been the greatest anchor to keep you captured by a previous season? How has that blocked your purpose to move forward?

If you were to begin moving forward today, what would that look like? What would you lose? Would it be worth it?

How has fear played a role in your trepidation of progress for your purpose?

From the Inside Out 12

MORNING MEDITATION

Psalm 51:10-12, New International Version

Create in me a pure heart, O God, and renew a steadfast spirit within me. Do not cast me from your presence or take your Holy Spirit from me. Restore to me the joy of your salvation and grant me a willing spirit, to sustain me.

EVENING DEVOTION

Psalm 119:9-16, New International Version

How can a young person stay on the path of purity? By living according to your word. I seek you with all my heart; do not let me stray from your commands. I have hidden your word in my heart that I might not sin against you. Praise be to you, Lord; teach me your decrees. With my lips I recount all the laws that come from your mouth. I rejoice in following your statutes as one rejoices in great riches. I meditate on your precepts and consider your ways. I delight in your decrees; I will not neglect your word.

One Sunday after church, my wife and I sat in the living room to relax. As we lounged, Ashriel came in followed by her two partners in crime. They had been in the garage searching for a pacifier, and we hadn't realized the amount of time that had transpired since their search began. As they walked in with heads hung low, Ashriel was carrying one of her mom's designer purses. "I didn't mean to!" were the first words out of her mouth.

The aroma of fingernail polish filled the room, and we quickly understood what happened. As Phineka began investigating the purse, she beheld pink nail polish splattered inside and outside it. All of the contents thereof had also been compromised by the accident.

I rubbed nail polish remover vigorously over the inside of the bag and just as the stains were starting to lift, my wife said something interesting, "Bae, don't worry about the inside of the purse. Nobody is going to see that. Just get the polish off the outside so I can still use it when I need it!" Her words may have been few, but they spoke volumes.

At some point or another, we have spent too much time fixing up our exterior so that the people we encounter will presume everything is going well. But on the inside, there was a massive explosion–a train wreck of sorts–which we attempted to hide for the sake of our reputation. Rather than taking the time to fix our wounded hearts, broken spirits, faulty faith, and more, we prefer to please people, maintain our personas, and suffer in silence. We don't consider that the interior damage is repairable if only we would allow transparency.

As you grow in your relationship with God, you will come to the point where you are transparent enough to say "these are the areas I need help with." Masks and façades only last as long as the wearer allows them to. In your life, you will come to the point where you realize that having things together on the outside while silently eroding on the inside is no longer an option. On the contrary, your desire must be for God to shape you from the inside out.

Internal work is challenging because it requires an honest assessment of who you are, where you have been, and where you are going. When you allow God to work on who you are, the masks become irrelevant; the façades no longer hold. When it is just you and God, there is only one answer that will stand: the truth. In this process, you will see your relationship with God mature because you are choosing heart work over head work.

Today, let God do surgery on your heart. Your purpose cannot be revealed through a façade. You deserve more. The world needs more. Open your heart and allow God to heal every broken area that has been hidden from the eyes of people. Open your mind and allow Him to remove any "stinking thinking." Open your spirit so He can move in and make you righteous. Allow Him to work on you from the inside out. When people see you, they will know that God has worked on your inside because it will shine through to the outside.

PURPOSE PRAYER

Heavenly Father,

I have tried to work on myself countless times and failed. I have let others work on me and they have fallen short. I have worn masks, kept up façades, and done everything possible to distract people from looking at me. Today, I put everything aside and open my heart to receive from You like never before. Give me a clean heart, pure thoughts, and an upright spirit so I can serve You. I give You permission to work on me from the inside out.

I declare that my heart is open and in need of the Ultimate Surgeon. I declare that every façade and mask I have used to hide the true condition of my heart is removed. I declare that as You work on me from the inside out, my mouth will sing Your praises and my lips will declare Your works. I declare that the world is waiting for me to be healed and I receive Your healing from the inside out.

In Jesus' Name, Amen.

PURPOSE FOCUS

What have you worked vigorously to clean on the outside while consistently ignoring the work God was trying to do on your soul?

What is the one thing in your heart that God has been nudging you about that has interfered with you pursuing purpose?

What have you still been holding that has been more of a burden to your purpose than a blessing to your current state?

13

You're Worth Something

MORNING MEDITATION

Psalm 139:13-18, New International Version

For you created my inmost being; you knit me together in my mother's womb. I praise you because I am fearfully and wonderfully made; your works are wonderful. I know that full well. My frame was not hidden from you when I was made in the secret place, when I was woven together in the depths of the earth. Your eyes saw my unformed body; all the days ordained for me were written in your book before one of them came to be. How precious to me are your thoughts, God! How vast is the sum of them! Were I to count them, they would outnumber the grains of sand–when I awake, I am still with you.

EVENING DEVOTION

Matthew 10:29-31, New International Version

Are not two sparrows sold for a penny? Yet not one of them will fall to the ground outside your Father's care. And even the very hairs of your head are all numbered. So don't be afraid; you are worth more than many sparrows.

I could not have asked for a more feminine batch of girls than the ones I have. They are miniatures of their mother. Each girl has her own unique persona, a desire for attention, and an understanding of her value and individuality. There is no better time to experience this display than Sunday mornings. As my wife preps the girls, their dialogue is always the same. Londyn will look at Ashriel and Amana and exclaim, "Ooooh! You look CUTE!" From there, a litany of adoration will transpire between the three. Though this behavior is most evident on Sunday mornings, Londyn has found a way to carry this self-admiration beyond Sunday. She is at the toddler stage of development where climbing is her delight. One day, I had the pleasure of watching her climb from the toilet seat to the bathroom counter so she could behold herself in the mirror. She began making a plethora of "cute" faces at herself. With hair untidy and wearing a onesie that had seen better days, she affirmed herself saying, "You sure are a cutie!" Though Londyn loves her Sunday morning appearances, she understands that her value and self-worth go deeper than what she wears.

Our greatest aspect of self-esteem, value, and worth is something deeper than what the world superficially calls beauty. Who you were created to be is so much more important! You were made in the image of God with a specific purpose and personality. Though it is easy to place value on clothes, makeup, jewelry, and other material items, it is more important to value the fact that God created us with great worth. When we understand our worth in God's eyes, our desire for affirmation from others will be viewed in a different light.

When we understand how valuable we are in God's eyes, we will never doubt His brilliant reasoning for creating us for such a time as this. You are worth something! Never forget it! When God created you, He intricately wove certain features into your make-up that are unique to you. Your individuality is not merely a cause to celebrate, but to thank God for being such an original Artist!

Your worth cannot only be attached to what you see externally. You must realize that on the worst of hair days, when your clothes don't match as well as they should, and even when you feel you don't look the part, the value God has placed in you never changes. God's investment in you goes deeper than your appearance. He invested purpose, destiny, and even Himself in you so you could become all that He created you to be!

Let your purpose in God be renewed and strengthened today by realizing that you are of great worth! When you gain a strong sense of value and refuse to settle for anything less, you will begin to gain an even greater appreciation for the purpose of God in your life. In the midst of this superficial world, remember that the seed of God's purpose is inside you. You were not born by mistake or mishap. God created you to live now and fulfill His plan for your life. Challenges will come to cause you to doubt your self-worth, but you are worth something. Never forget it. Value yourself and realize you are worth more than anything this world can offer!

PURPOSE PRAYER

Heavenly Father,

I was created in Your Image with value that goes beyond my wildest imaginations. I am valuable. Lord, help me to value myself as much as You do and to put aside the worldly ideas that cause me to discredit Your creative expertise in my life. I am valuable because You say I am and that is worth more than anything this world can offer. Thank You for creating me in Your image!

I declare that I am fearfully and wonderfully made. I declare that I am made in Your image and likeness. I declare that every obstacle that comes to attack my self-worth will be a building block to help me become all that You desire me to be. I declare that in the face of a world obsessed with superficial values, my worth is rooted in You and Your purpose for creating me. I declare that I am worth something!

In Jesus' Name, Amen.

PURPOSE FOCUS

How do you really feel about you? How has that reflection helped or hurt you pursue purpose?

Who or what caused the greatest damage to your self-esteem and self-worth? What has kept you from getting over it?

When was the last time you intentionally sought to see yourself from His perspective?

The Boyfriend Saga 14

MORNING DEVOTION

Ecclesiastes 2:24-26, New International Version

A person can do nothing better than to eat and drink and find satisfaction in their own toil. This too, I see, is from the hand of God, for without him, who can eat or find enjoyment? To the person who pleases him, God gives wisdom, knowledge and happiness, but to the sinner he gives the task of gathering and storing up wealth to hand it over to the one who pleases God. This too is meaningless, a chasing after the wind.

EVENING DEVOTION

Romans 12:1-2, New International Version

Therefore, I urge you, brothers and sisters, in view of God's mercy, to offer your bodies as a living sacrifice, holy and pleasing to God—this is your true and proper worship. Do not conform to the pattern of this world, but be transformed by the renewing of your mind. Then you will be able to test and approve what God's will be—his good, pleasing and perfect will.

Londyn has a boyfriend. Yes, my three-year-old proudly came home from preschool one day and announced that her heart had been taken by a young boy in her class named "Alex." Every time she says his name, she bats her eyelashes in excitement because he is so "in love" with her. Her teachers, much to my chagrin, love the fact that they have their first preschool couple of the year and make sure they sit together in class each day. It is a father's worst nightmare come true.

The conversation about Alex quickly turned into an everyday comedic drama. He always did something different to make her love him more. It started off with small hugs and then quickly escalated to a kiss on the back of her shirt. A week later, they were giving each other full-fledged kisses on the lips before they left school each day. As I would pick her up, his dad and I would simply exchange looks and shake our heads. We both knew what the other was experiencing at home because of this toddler romance.

One day, I decided to test Londyn's allegiance to me by giving her a very challenging request. I sat her on my lap and told her I wanted her to break up with Alex. The conversation went back and forth for several minutes until she finally said, "Daddy, if you want me to break up with Alex, I will. I just want you to be happy."

As much as these words melted my heart, I knew somewhere in the back of my mind that the tables would turn against me if I didn't allow this puppy love to play out. Thankfully, Alex moved away before the opportunity for any serious dating arose. Alex was a great kid, trust me. I love him even more from a distance than I did in close proximity. All kidding aside, Londyn's response to my challenge spoke volumes. She made it clear that she would do whatever I wanted to her to because she wanted her daddy to be pleased. We would do well to take notes from her. We should live our lives completely emptied out in order to please the Father in everything we say and do.

When we live our lives for an audience of One, what we do becomes less performance-based and more purpose-based. It's almost too easy to get caught in the trap of living to satisfy others without consulting the Father to see what His desires are for us. Pleasing people becomes a challenge because their desires can change on a daily basis; the moods of the masses are inconsistent and utterly changeable.

Living for God wholeheartedly and ignoring the will of others positions us to see God's divine will unfold in our lives like never before. When we take ourselves entirely out of the equation and silence the voices of others, we are then able to clearly hear what pleases the heart of God. In fact, we will never be satisfied as long as we choose popularity over purpose. Pleasing people provides only limited fulfillment. Pleasing God comes with a lifetime of benefits.

Is God really concerned about the minor aspects of your life? Absolutely! Everything about you creates the path to fulfilling your destiny. From the smallest to the greatest of us, God is concerned about us and desires to be pleased with the lives we lead. When you live wholeheartedly for God, the reward is greater than anything this world can offer.

Just as Londyn struggled with her own decision, we too will encounter challenging decisions when we decide to follow God wholeheartedly. There are times when pleasing God completely dissatisfies our fleshly desires. At the end of the day, we were created by Him, for His pleasure, to fulfill His will in the earth. When we put ourselves aside and consider the privilege of serving God, we quickly remember the importance and benefits of dying to self.

You are on the path to purpose. Don't allow small distractions to contaminate your everyday progress in fulfilling His plan for your life. You are on the right track. Keep moving ahead!

PURPOSE PRAYER

Heavenly Father,

There are days when I honestly struggle choosing between my will and Yours. Teach me every day that trusting and submitting to You is the best decision I can ever make. Don't allow me to get distracted by what the world offers. Instead, let my life be completely immersed in fulfilling Your purpose and plan for my life.

I declare that my heart belongs to You. I declare that my heart and mind are ruled by You. I declare that everything that seeks to distract me from the course of purpose is exposed and eradicated from my life. I declare that no matter what comes my way, my heart will always belong to You first. Thank You for loving me with an everlasting love!

In Jesus' Name, Amen.

PURPOSE FOCUS

Are you more content with pleasing people than the audience of One? How does your daily life reflect your response?

Are you still wired to perform for a response than to completely live in purpose? Do you seek applause or affirmation from heaven?

When was the last time you abandoned people and opinions completely to pursue purpose?

15

Cleaning up the Mess

MORNING MEDITATION

Psalm 1:1-3, New Revised Standard Version

Happy are those who do not follow the advice of the wicked, or take the path that sinners tread, or sit in the seat of scoffers; but their delight is in the law of the LORD, and on his law they meditate day and night. They are like trees planted by streams of water, which yield their fruit in its season, and their leaves do not wither. In all that they do, they prosper.

EVENING DEVOTION

Hebrews 12:1-3, New Revised Standard Version

Therefore, since we are surrounded by such a great cloud of witnesses, let us throw off everything that hinders and the sin that so easily entangles. And let us run with perseverance the race marked out for us, fixing our eyes on Jesus, the pioneer and perfecter of faith. For the joy set before him he endured the cross, scorning its shame, and sat down at the right hand of the throne of God. Consider him who endured such opposition from sinners, so that you will not grow weary and lose heart.

During Christmas 2010, my family prepared to move back to Alabama. On one particular night, all five of us (at the time) had to pile into one queen size bed to sleep because of the intense packing. (Thankfully, no small children were harmed in this process.) The following morning, I woke up before everyone to finish clearing out my daughters' rooms before they woke. During a break, I went to check on everyone since I presumed they were still asleep.

Before I could open the door, I was met by an "aroma." Now this wasn't your average household smell. It was something I could have lived my whole life without smelling. Lying in my bed were two–count 'em–TWO diapers soiled with "number two." The smell was horrific! Everyone was resting peacefully. I woke Phineka up, borderline fussing, because I couldn't understand how she could sleep in the room with such a stench. As she rubbed her eyes, stretching from her sleep, she said, "Bay, I don't smell anything." I looked at her in utter shock and disbelief as she left the room to get some orange juice.

As I debated which baby's booty to tackle first, my wife walked back in with juice in hand. Upon reentry, she sat her cup down and quickly covered her nose in disgust. Her testimony had changed. Instead of being oblivious to what I'd smelled from the beginning, she looked at me cross-eyed and said, "Bay, I see what you were talking about!" She had been in the same room as the odor for so long that what should have offended her seemed normal. Her closeness over time created a familiarity with the smell. It prevented her from reacting the way she typically would have.

There are moments in your life when you have been surrounded by "smells" for so long that they no longer bother you. Those on the outside have the ability to sense that something is wrong, yet we miss the problem completely until we step away and reevaluate the situation.

When we refuse to recognize that some of our company and conversations are driving us further away from God, we find ourselves in the same spiritual, emotional, and mental stalemates. We will consistently feel like we are not accomplishing anything and living a life of mediocrity. We must come to the point where we desire to see a change in our surroundings. When we know that there is a possibility to achieve better in our lives, we must pursue better relentlessly.

As you renew your pursuit of God and His will for your life, you will be forced to evaluate every area of your life. Stepping away to take a second look is the difference between triumph and demise. Just because you have always handled people a certain way doesn't mean that you should continue to do so. Just because you have always handled your finances a certain way doesn't mean that it is the most advantageous for you. A proper evaluation of your life requires a renewed perspective, free from the stench of experience, and strengthened by the encouragement of God's Word.

As you seek to grow in your relationship with God, you must also properly assess each relationship in your life. It is imperative that you check every "room" in your life to make sure there are no "odors." What "stench" has become so familiar in your life that it causes you to mistakenly smell fresh-cut roses instead of raw sewage? There is no better time than now to reevaluate everything that has the potential to cloud your mind or impede your judgment.

Right now is a pivotal moment in your life. Don't let stinky situations dictate your decisions. Decide to throw out the trash, change the diapers, or whatever it takes to regain control over your life. Don't risk missing the greatness God has for you because you refused to address the smelly situations in your life. You were destined for greatness. Decide to make it come to pass.

PURPOSE PRAYER

Heavenly Father,

I have experienced stinky situations in my life, but I refuse to let them consume me. Today, I make a conscious decision to reevaluate every area of my life. I trust You to reveal everything that needs to be uncovered in my heart. I trust You to be my Revealer and Healer. Show me what I need to know and heal me from what may break my heart. I'm cleaning up the mess and starting anew!

Today, I declare that I seek You and Your Kingdom first in all things and do not follow the advice of the wicked. I declare that I follow in the steps You've ordered for my life and do not walk in the steps of sinners. I declare that I treat others the way You treat me and do not sit in the seat of mockers. I declare that with Your help, I will clean up every mess in my life so that I will become all You desire for me to be.

In Jesus' Name, Amen.

PURPOSE FOCUS

Have you become more familiar with the stench of your situation than the Savior who redeemed you from it?

Are you still holding over your head situations that you cannot change? How has that impeded your pursuit of purpose?

Who have you let in to help you clean your mess?

16

Let's Work Together

MORNING MEDITATION

Ecclesiastes 4:9-12, New International Version

Two are better than one, because they have a good return for their labor: If either of them falls down, one can help the other up. But pity anyone who falls and has no one to help them up. Also, if two lie down together, they will keep warm. But how can one keep warm alone? Though one may be overpowered, two can defend themselves. A cord of three strands is not quickly broken.

EVENING DEVOTION

I Corinthians 12:12-14, New International Version

Just as a body, though one, has many parts, but all its many parts form one body, so it is with Christ. For we were all baptized by one Spirit so as to form one body–whether Jews or Gentiles, slave or free–and we were all given the one Spirit to drink. Even so the body is not made up of one part but of many.

My wife and I love spying on the girls during their playtime. Don't get me wrong, it's not that creepy kind of spying that would make you feel uncomfortable or wonder what the heck is wrong with us. It's the type of spying that allows us to enjoy watching our kids play, interact, and solve their own conflicts. We decided early on that we wanted the girls, even at a young age, to realize their need for one another and learn to help each other.

One particular afternoon, the trio was playing in the backyard. As they played, the infamous fight over toys began. Londyn and Amana were fighting over a ball. Amana was on the verge of lying on the turf to commence a tantrum. We watched peeking through the blinds. As my wife prepared to intervene, Ashriel began mediating the situation. She stepped in as the two younger girls were beginning to wear themselves out and proceeded to give them "the speech." As she lectured them, their eyes focused on her with intense concern. Though we couldn't hear everything she said, we heard her end with this statement: "We are sisters, and we need each other. We have to share because we love each other and we all need to be happy!" A few moments later, they were all sitting on the turf rolling the ball back and forth as if nothing had ever happened.

God created us to be unique individuals. Built within our individuality is the need for agreement, support, love, and acceptance from those with whom we are close. Ultimately, a major portion of our growth in God has to do with how we treat people. When God's love is in our heart, our desire is always to live in peace, harmony, and love with our brothers and sisters in Christ. We seek to resolve conflicts and keep our emotions together even at the most challenging of times. We consider others over our own needs, wants, and desires. We want to see the love of God on display as much as possible.

No individual is an island unto himself. God created us with an inherent need to desire peaceful relationships with others. When we attempt to live life by ourselves, we miss out on the benefits of having someone else experience the journey and create memories with us along the way. These benefits will last much longer than they would have had they been attained alone.

We were created to be interdependent, relying upon each another. There was a reason God refused to leave Adam alone in the Garden of Eden: he needed companionship. He needed someone with whom to experience life. He needed someone who could understand him and communicate the same way. God wired us the same way, and we honestly live better when we choose to work with each other.

Just as our bodies would never work properly if every part were the same, so will our lives never work properly or be complete if we attempt to do everything on our own. Our personal independence can never erase our need for relationships. Our hearts can never be so closed off to outside assistance that we miss the people God is attempting to bring into our lives who will help us transition to the next place of purpose.

Working together doesn't mean that you will get along with everyone all the time. However, it does mean that there is a continual pursuit of a common goal. It means that the unity of this goal is greater than individual personalities or agendas.

When the girls were in the middle of their dispute, Ashriel saw the big picture. She didn't want to deal with a big argument and the consequences thereof. Instead, she chose to bring everyone present to a place of agreement. When we decide to work together, we will always keep the bigger goal of peace, harmony, and unity in mind so we can fulfill all of our godly desires.

You may have blocked people from your heart and life for one reason or another, but you need people the same way you need progress in life. Don't separate yourself from a healthy dependence on people. Ask God daily to reveal the individuals assigned to your life so you can achieve your purpose in His timing. Living in purpose is so much better when you do it with others!

PURPOSE PRAYER

Heavenly Father,

I know that I need people to help me get where I need to go even though my ultimate faith and trust is in You. Help me to let down the walls of my heart that have caused me to fail in my attempts to let others know I need them in my life. Teach me to work with others the same way You work with me.

I declare that my purpose will be released through individuals willing to partner with me. I declare that my walls fall and that I grasp the opportunity to engage with others in order to bring Your will to fruition in my life and the lives of others. I declare that I will walk in agreement with those who are around me so I can truly fulfill all that You have for my life.

In Jesus' Name, Amen.

PURPOSE FOCUS

Do you understand your need for others in your life? What keeps you from allowing people in?

How can the right people and voices complement your purpose today?

Have senseless disputes left you void of the right voices to move your life forward?

17

Addicted No More

MORNING MEDITATION

Psalm 30:4-5, New Revised Standard Version

Sing praises to the LORD, O you his faithful ones, and give thanks to his holy name. For his anger is but for a moment; his favor is for a lifetime. Weeping may linger for the night, but joy comes with the morning.

EVENING DEVOTION

Hebrews 12:1-2, New Revised Standard Version

Therefore, since we are surrounded by so great a cloud of witnesses, let us also lay aside every weight and the sin that clings so closely, and let us run with perseverance the race that is set before us, looking to Jesus the pioneer and perfecter of our faith, who for the sake of the joy that was set before him endured the cross, disregarding its shame, and has taken his seat at the right hand of the throne of God.

All children go through stages where there is something they hold tightly for security purposes. For some, it is a teddy bear or small object they adore. For others, it may be a person they have grown to favor over time. For my daughter, Amana, the object of her affection was a pacifier.

It would have been okay if Amana sucked her pacifier only on certain occasions, but the best word I can use to explain her attachment is addiction. When I say "addiction," I mean that she had to have it morning, noon, and night. She became a master at eating with it still lodged in the side of her cheek. She attempted full-fledged conversations while still clinging to her "pappy." Somehow, she even figured out a way to drink milk and still keep her pacifier plugged in at the same time.

I remember days when we would cut holes in her pacifiers and let her know that she was a "big girl" now and no longer needed them. She would go through all of the motions of throwing them in the garbage with us, clapping her hands in excitement, and moving on temporarily with the functions of her day. Before long, she would be found rummaging through the garbage in search of a pacifier or crying until we went to the store to purchase another one.

The addiction finally broke after Layel was born. We coached her on how Layel needed pacifiers now and that she could be a big helper by letting them go. Though the first days were challenging, slowly but surely, the pacifier stronghold began to break. She would ask for it and then remind herself, "I'm a big girl now." We watched through the weeks as her vocabulary became clearer and improved without the pacifier impeding her conversation. Now, the pacifier is a thing of the past that is only brought up in the context of babies.

What is amazing about life and fulfilling purpose is that there are days and moments when we simply have to realize that the things we thought we needed are not as important or valuable as they once were. In truth, it is possible to allow things that we believe we need to become crutches that keep us from progressing the way we should. When we are faced with these types of mountains or milestones, we must decide whether we will let go and move on or maintain our hold and make little progress, if any at all.

What has become your "pacifier" in life? What are you still holding for all the wrong reasons? The tragedy of the pacifier is that when a child uses it for too long, it causes their entire dental structure to grow out of alignment. There are things lingering in your life trying to destroy your divine alignment with God and prevent you from fulfilling your purpose. The sooner you allow these things to be removed, the sooner you can refocus and fulfill your purpose.

Some things are okay for a season, but when that season expires, it is necessary to release the possession, paradigm, or person to move forward. They do more harm than good when allowed to linger beyond their allotted time in your life. Honestly, things that once appeared to be a blessing in your life can quickly turn into a burden if not released at the right time. Do not allow your purpose to be burdened by holding on to the wrong thing far longer than you should.

At the end of the day, the question is quite simple: how badly do you want what's next for you in life? How badly do you want to achieve your purpose? You cannot receive God's best without releasing what has expired in your life. We will all face the challenging crossroad where letting go is not just the best option, but the only option to move forward in destiny and purpose. It may hurt now, but it will hurt more if you remain in a place longer than you should.

When Amana began to break her habit, there were days she would cry for her lost pappy. Pretty soon, her tears turned into faint memories of what once was. It is amazing how the things we cry about today become the things we forget tomorrow. Do not allow the temporary pain of releasing what was once valuable to keep you from moving forward. Hurt is temporary, but joy lasts forever.

Weeping may last for a moment, but the ultimate joy of pleasing God and releasing that which holds you back far outweighs the bad. Today, take a moment to consider the things–and people–that you have allowed to hang around in your life. Have they been more of a detriment than a help in achieving your God-ordained purpose? If so, do not be afraid to proclaim, "I am addicted no more!"

PURPOSE PRAYER

Heavenly Father,

I know there are situations that I have allowed to linger in my heart and mind far longer than they should. I have given the enemy a foothold in my life by allowing him to play on my heart and mind as it pertains to releasing the things which attempt to stop my purpose. No matter how small or great my addiction is, today I choose to let go.

I declare that nothing will stop me from releasing what has expired in my life so I can receive God's best for my future! I declare that the temporary pain I will experience cannot be compared to the joy of moving forward. I declare that for the rest of my life, I will be motivated about keeping every distraction out of my heart and life that would be detrimental to fulfilling God's plan for my life!

In Jesus' Name, Amen.

PURPOSE FOCUS

What are you clinging to that has literally stood in the way of your purpose?

Do you recognize when something has expired in your life? How do you manage the moments when seasons change?

Do you believe that it is possible for you to outgrow a thing? Is there something you are still holding that you should have released a long time ago?

18

It's a New Day

MORNING MEDITATION

Isaiah 43:18-21, New International Version

Do not remember the former things, nor consider the things of old. Behold, I will do a new thing, now it shall spring forth; shall you not know it? I will even make a road in the wilderness and rivers in the desert. The beast of the field will honor Me, the jackals and the ostriches, because I give waters in the wilderness and rivers in the desert, to give drink to My people, My chosen. This people I have formed for Myself; They shall declare My praise.

EVENING DEVOTION

II Corinthians 5:16-19, New International Version

So from now on we regard no one from a worldly point of view. Though we once regarded Christ in this way, we do so no longer. Therefore, if anyone is in Christ, the new creation has come: The old has gone, the new is here! All this is from God, who reconciled us to himself through Christ and gave us the ministry of reconciliation: that God was reconciling the world to himself in Christ, not counting people's sins against them. And he has committed to us the message of reconciliation.

Anytime we go out for groceries or even to get gas, it is almost a guarantee that one of the "little people" who tag along with us will ask for something. It could be something they legitimately need, but more often than not, it's something they would not have considered had we not taken the trip. When at all possible, we try to leave anyone under five feet tall at home on shopping trips.

One weekend while Phineka was on bed rest, I had the all-important responsibility of taking the girls to a birthday party. Being the brave dad I am, I decided that it would be safe to wait until we were en route to the party to get the birthday girl a gift. We stopped in Toys R' Us, and that was when things took a turn for the worse.

"Daddy, I need this!"

"Daddy, have you ever seen one of these?"

"Daddy, I need one!"

"Daddy! Amana said I could have this. Is that okay?"

The litany of inquiries and responses went on for fifteen minutes until I finally caved in, purchased everyone a small trinket, and ran for the door as fast as possible. They were all smiles in the backseat as we drove to the party because everyone got something new.

Believe it or not, today is completely new to you. This is a day you have never seen before and when it passes, you will never see it again. God has granted you this day to embrace a new opportunity and purpose for your life. How can I be so certain? Simple: You're reading this devotional. Every new day is an opportunity to embrace new opportunities, new perspectives, and new horizons for your life. Ultimately, you have a new day today because God is ready to do a new thing in your heart and life!

To properly understand that, we must first know that nothing is ever new to God. How can something be new to the One who knows everything? However, there will always be new things for us to embrace as God chooses to reveal them to us. When God does a new thing, that means He is ready to show us some things concerning Him that we have yet to experience in our lives.

There are two things God requires for us to receive the fullness of this new day for our lives: forgetting the past and refusing ever to consider it again. I've discovered that in life, our experience has more influence on our future than we would like to give it credit. At times, we maintain walls and guards against people because of what we experienced in past relationships. We have all experienced fear when stepping out on a new plan God has given us because of a previous failure. God tells us specifically through the Prophet Isaiah that His desire is to do something new and in order for us to receive it, we must forget "stuff." In other words, to receive the new "stuff," we must be willing to forget the old.

Once God starts the new thing, He says that it will quickly come forward in your life. It is similar to planting a seed in the ground. When the seed is first planted, you do not see anything but the dirt that you placed on top of it. Before you know it, that small seed is a small plant beginning to bud out of the ground. It was a process that required patience, but it came to pass nonetheless. God states here that when He starts the new thing, we will see an immediate response to His actions. The word "now" denotes that the new thing is immediate. Just like when God spoke and created the earth everything came into place immediately, so it is with us today as God declares a new thing.

As you keep your heart in God's hand, there will be numerous opportunities for you to embrace purpose and experience newness in your relationship with Him.

Yesterday is gone, today is here, and tomorrow is coming. Don't let errors from yesterday paralyze your progress for today and abort your purpose for tomorrow. This is a new day for you in God! Old things have passed away. As you grow in your understanding of God's plan for your life, He will continue to refresh you with the newness that comes from Him. Yes, this is a new day for your life, and the best is yet to come!

PURPOSE PRAYER

Heavenly Father,

Today I choose to forget the pain of my yesterday and focus wholeheartedly on the promise of my tomorrow. Mistakes have been made, but today, my heart is repentant of what was and is completely focused on what is to come. My heart is free, my mind is open, and my spirit is receptive to the new things that You desire to reveal in my life!

I declare that I embrace new opportunities with optimism and faith in Your plans for my life. I declare that the hold that yesterday had on my heart and mind is released so that I can become all that You desire for me to be. I declare that I walk in the fulfillment of my purpose and that this day is simply a new opportunity for me to embrace it.

In Jesus' Name, Amen.

PURPOSE FOCUS

What "new" has God been trying to show you for your life? How does it have the ability to enhance your purpose?

Have you been cautious of God sending you something that you didn't ask for? Do you equate His blessings with your own personal work/worth?

Do you still penalize your future because of mistakes from your past? How so?

What's in Your Heart? 19

MORNING DEVOTION

Proverbs 4:23, New Revised Standard Version

Keep your heart with all vigilance, for from it flows the springs of life.

EVENING DEVOTION

Luke 6:43-45, New Revised Standard Version

No good tree bears bad fruit, nor again does a bad tree bear good fruit; for each tree is known by its own fruit. Figs are not gathered from thorns, nor are grapes picked from a bramble bush. The good person out of the good treasure of the heart produces good, and the evil person out of the veil treasure produces evil; for it is out of the abundance of the heart that the mouth speaks.

Out of all four girls, Ashriel is the biggest social butterfly. There are few settings in which she doesn't find herself engaging in conversation or interacting with others. Whether in a church, on the plane, or even in the restroom (so I've heard), she'll find a way to strike up a conversation with her new friends.

This would be problematic for some, but Phineka and I have learned to embrace this aspect of Ashriel because of how she goes about it. Whenever she meets someone, she almost always does so by complimenting them. From loving someone's color coordination and accessories to the ringlets in their hair, compliments are definitely one of Ashriel's strongest suits.

Ashriel does so freely because it's a true expression of her heart. There is nothing fake or phony about it. Ever since she was a toddler, she has always had a heart for people. She loves making them feel good about themselves and uses whatever means she can to do so. This is such a free-flowing part of her personality that instead of seeing it as strange or even interesting, we understand that it is an expression of her heart.

It's very interesting that Scripture often reminds us to guard our hearts and what flows from them. Our heart is the seat of our emotions and can be influenced by the situations that transpire in our lives. What our hearts feel, our minds think, and our mouths speak. When our hearts have been broken, hurt, or ill-used by others, it can cause us to view people and life through the lens of brokenness.

Furthermore, when our hearts don't heal properly and are filled with anger, bitterness, negativity, jealousy, and so on, it not only affects us internally, but externally. Can you think of a person you always attempt to avoid because of their constant negativity, bitterness, or anger? When we refuse to allow God to heal our hearts properly, we open ourselves to the possibility of injury caused by our interactions with the world.

What makes Ashriel's expression so endearing is that it's pure. When our hearts are pure, others will recognize it. Our motives will never be questioned because they'll be obvious. People will know that we are speaking, giving, and loving from a place of purity.

Your purpose will never be fulfilled while you hold on to the pain of your past. Even when you attempt to ignore the circumstances of your past, it is almost a guarantee that those around you will pick up on your pain without you ever verbalizing it. You may be able to fool people for a short period of time with words, but eventually, your heart will be exposed through your actions. Broken hearts always speak from broken places. Today, there is a call for you to move forward in life, but you can't move ahead while looking back. When Jesus presented parables about trees and their fruit, He made several things clear. We are known by the fruit we bear. People know your heart because it is revealed through your words and actions. The reality is clear. You can't say one thing and be something else. Your reputation is based on the words your heart speaks.

Today, take a bold step and search the contents of your heart. Be honest enough to deal with your present realities while remaining motivated enough to take positive steps in the right direction. If and when you realize that your heart has been filled with something that's been causing you to shrink back from the purpose of God for you, don't run away from it. Deal with it head on and expect God to do a work of healing in your heart and life. When you are bold enough to accept your flaws and failures, you will also be bold enough to uproot anything that has been growing in your life that would prevent you from moving forward in a healthy way.

PURPOSE PRAYER

Heavenly Father,

I understand that there have been places in my heart that have been hurt or broken by situations in life. I want to be healed mentally, emotionally, and spiritually of every wound that has caused my heart to be broken. I want to walk in complete healing and total freedom in every area of my life. I want the flow of my heart to be pure and in line with God's will.

I declare that my heart is healed. I declare that the negativity, bitterness, anger, jealousy, frustration, and more that have attempted to rob me of my purpose are removed from my life. I declare that since my heart is healed, my purpose is renewed and I walk in power and victory in every area of my life. My declaration is clear: I am healed!

In Jesus' Name, Amen.

PURPOSE FOCUS

If God were to do open heart surgery to expose to the world everything in it, what would we find?

How have the contents of your heart hindered your purpose in times past? What do you run the risk of repeating because of unaddressed damage from yesterday?

Who really holds the key to your heart and future? Can they be trusted?

20

I Need You

MORNING MEDITATION

Psalm 42:1-5, New Revised Standard Version

As a deer longs for flowing streams, so my soul longs for you, O God. My soul thirsts for God, for the living God. When shall I come and behold the face of God? My tears have been my food day and night, while people say to me continually, "Where is your God?" These things I remember, as I pour out my soul: how I went with the throng, and led them in procession to the house of God, with glad shouts and songs of thanksgiving, a multitude keeping festival. Why are you cast down, O my soul, and why are you disquieted within me? Hope in God; for I shall again praise him, my help and my God.

EVENING DEVOTION

Jeremiah 29:11-14, New Revised Standard Version

For surely I know the plans I have for you, says the LORD, plans for your welfare and not for harm, to give you a future with hope. Then when you call upon me and come and pray to me, I will hear you. When you search for me, you will find me; if you seek me with all your heart, I will let you find me, says the LORD, and I will restore your fortunes and gather you from all the nations and all the places where I have driven you, says the LORD, and I will bring you back to the place from which I sent you into exile.

After the birth of our last daughter, Layel, we had to readjust our lives to the needs of an infant all over again. Life had become somewhat balanced with each of our older daughters having their respective amounts of independence and capabilities. They would play throughout the house at their leisure and come to us only to "tattle" on each other. We did not have the concern of changing diapers, feeding and sleeping schedules, and everything else that comes with caring for an infant. It was an interesting development in our household, to say the least.

What I discovered about Layel was that she was not as concerned about what's going on in our lives as she was about having her needs met. She did not care if Phineka was cooking dinner or helping Ashriel with homework. If she was hungry, she demanded to eat immediately. She did not care if it was three in the afternoon or three in the morning; if her diaper needed changing, she wanted it done immediately. If we happened to be a minute late or a bit short of her request, she let us all know through many tears and screams for attention.

As Layel continued to develop, she learned certain signs and actions she could make to get our attention quickly. She could not talk yet, but she learned that if she whined just the right way, we would run to her to figure out what's wrong. She knew what to do to make us move on her behalf. As an infant, she learned her parents enough to know that there are just certain things she needs us to do for her. If we didn't do it for her, it wouldn't happen. After discovering this, she didn't waste any time letting us know when she had a need. There is not a place in our lives and relationship with God where He does not require total dependence on Him. We will never get to a place in life where we can say, "I don't need God anymore." Instead, the more we mature in Him, the more we understand that every aspect of our lives is entirely dependent upon His guidance, presence, and power.

Purpose is found when we stop searching for our way and completely depend on God. We cannot trust our choices or knowledge to bring us to a place that can only be found in the depths of God. We must pursue Him relentlessly to experience His presence every moment of our lives. The more we depend on Him, the less we depend on ourselves and those around us to make decisions that God understands better than any of us ever could.

Our desire to know God is centered on seeking Him with our whole hearts. Growing in purpose and relationship with God has nothing to do with half-hearted attempts and everything to do with wholeheartedly chasing after Him. God does not want part of us; He wants all of us. As we seek Him with all that is in us, He will guide us according to His Word and will for our lives.

Just as Layel screamed for her parents' attention, there is a place where we as children of God have the ability to cry out to Him for direction, assistance, and divine intervention in our lives. Even when we allow ourselves to get into self-induced messes, His desire is not for us to stay messy forever. He wants us to be in a place where we are living in purpose, walking in power, and fulfilling His plan for our lives with the guidance of His Spirit in everything we do. When we submit our will to His, He will always lead us down the correct path for our lives.

Our Father is concerned about every aspect of our lives. He is the epitome of a true Father. Consequently, we must come to the point where we trust Him enough to cast all the worries of our world at His feet. He knows exactly what we need, when we need it, which is why we must be completely dependent on Him. He understands the purpose of our lives. In everything, God's request for us is to completely trust Him to provide all of our needs. He will come through. He will do what He promised. Today, grow more in your walk with God by realizing your utter dependence on Him for every aspect of your life.

PURPOSE PRAYER

Heavenly Father,

On my own, I do not have a clue of what direction my life should go. With You, my life fits together like puzzle pieces. Thank You for being the Guide of my life and for giving me the ability to completely depend on You no matter what happens.

I declare that I will not be more dependent on people than I am on You. I declare that You are the God Who provides for every area of my life and I trust You to do what You do best. I declare that my wisdom does not compare to Yours and I will trust Your way above my own. I declare that I will stop trying to control every area of my life and allow You to guide me according to Your will. I am dependent on You!

In Jesus' Name, Amen.

PURPOSE FOCUS

Have you learned the power of complete dependence on God?

Do your current accomplishments amount to complete dependence on Him?

In what ways are you still relying on your ability more than His?

21

Anywhere, but Backward

MORNING MEDITATION

Philippians 3:12-14, New International Version

Not that I have already obtained all this, or have already arrived at my goal, but I press on to take hold of that for which Christ Jesus took hold of me. Brothers and sisters, I do not consider myself yet to have taken hold of it. But one thing I do: Forgetting what is behind and straining toward what is ahead, I press on toward the goal to win the prize for which God has called me heavenward in Christ Jesus.

EVENING DEVOTION

I Peter 2:1-3, New International Version

Therefore, rid yourselves of all malice and all deceit, hypocrisy, envy, and slander of every kind. Like newborn babies, crave pure spiritual milk, so that by it you may grow up in your salvation, now that you have tasted that the Lord is good.

Quite naturally, Layel has grown by leaps and bounds since birth. It started with large motor skills such as holding up her head, sticking her fingers in her mouth, etc. As the months progressed, she began sitting up on her own, rolling over from back to stomach, and everything else that came with that.

Her proudest accomplishment, however, was one she learned in the early stages of crawling. With the encouragement of her sisters, she would raise up her small body from the floor and "scoot" on her hands and knees.

Her excitement and laughter over this personal feat often caused her to fall more than she crawled, but she was just excited about her overall mobility.

There was just one problem with her scooting. She only went one direction–backward. Yes, all of her joy and excitement was over her ability to go in the wrong direction. Though her sisters tried to tell her she needed to go forward, her attempts always took her in the opposite direction. Even with Amana getting down on all fours and modeling how to scoot forward, she still insisted on going backward.

It's not that she couldn't move forward. We watched her slowly inch ahead when she chose to. She just liked to go backward. It brought her delight to see the faces urging her in one direction while she went in the other. Thankfully, this was a very short stage in her life!

Layel's crawling situation represents where many people find themselves in life - always moving backward and never forward. The challenge is to no longer live in the past so they can walk into the future God has ordained for their lives. When we are constantly looking and moving backward, we can never focus on what He desires to do in the now situations of our lives.

Backward cannot be an option in your life. You must come to the point where you are bold enough to say it, speak it, and believe it for your own life. When you recognize the significance of God's call and plan for your life, you will understand that wallowing in the past will only prevent you from attaining your future. You must come to a significant moment in which you embrace what happened, own it as a part of your life experience, and see the hand of God working through it to navigate you through the next steps of life.

Backward is not just a challenge caused by negative experiences. It is also caused by great accomplishments we prefer to relive instead of moving forward. We can get stuck celebrating the past milestones of life to such a degree that we do not embrace the opportunities set before us. It is impossible to move into the future while reliving the past. This is not to say that the accomplishment was not worthy of honor, yet you will never go to your next while reveling in the glory of what was.

We typically "scoot" backward when we are faced with opposition that challenges our will to go forward. We think about how good things could have been if we had done this or that. We consider how our lives would have been different if this or that had not transpired. We attempt to look at circumstances that, no matter how long we think on them, will never change. We must resolve that what we have experienced was for our benefit and that through it all, God can help us move forward.

By refusing to go backward, you resolve that your purpose will never get stuck in the memory of what was. When you know that God's plan for you is greater than your past, you will hunger and thirst for your future in Him. Your past is your past for a reason. Let this be the day you release yourself from reliving memories and choose to see the purpose of God revealed through your life in the new experiences He has for you.

PURPOSE PRAYER

Heavenly Father,

There have been times in my life when I focused too much on what happened and not enough on how you worked it out for my good. Today, I know that You are calling me to a future that can only be orchestrated by Your hand on my life. With that in mind, I know I can move beyond my past and never look back again.

I declare that in the midst of my greatest challenges in life, backward will never be an option. I declare that I am free from my past and any pain that may have been incurred by it so that I can walk in full liberty as the person You created me to be. I declare that I will not live in the victories of yesterday and that I will climb the mountains to access my tomorrow. I declare that through every challenge, I will still give God praise for helping me move forward.

In Jesus' Name, Amen.

PURPOSE FOCUS

Have you become more satisfied with your past accomplishments than your future pursuits?

How have you hindered your purpose by gazing in the rear view mirror of what was?

What have you held on to as a trophy from your history that has disrupted God's future plans for your life?

22

Pick Me Up

MORNING MEDITATION

Psalm 3:1-4, New Revised Standard Version

O Lord, how many are my foes! Many are rising against me; many are saying to me, "There is no help for you in God." Selah but you, O Lord, are a shield around me, my glory, and the one who lifts up my head. I cry aloud to the Lord, and he answers me from his holy hill. Selah

EVENING DEVOTION

Isaiah 41:8-10, New Revised Standard Version

But you, Israel, my servant, Jacob, whom I have chosen, the offspring of Abraham, my friend; you whom I took from the ends of the earth, and called from its farthest corners, saying to you, "You are my servant, I have chosen you and not cast you off"; do not fear, for I am with you, do not be afraid, for I am your God; I will strengthen you, I will help you, I will uphold you with my victorious right hand.

In our home, night duty is known as the late hours of the night and wee hours of the morning when our children make requests that require an immediate response from a parent. My wife resigned from all such services about a while ago which meant that the brunt of that responsibility fell on me. The number of night duty requests typically varied. Some nights, there was only one.

Whenever Londyn wandered into our room in the middle of the night, there were certain things she required before her request could be fulfilled. You see, when she left her room for ours, she had to walk through a dark hallway and living room to get to the other side of the house. By the time she arrived in our room, she was normally already in tears, not just because she wanted something to drink, but because she hated being alone in the dark. So before we could begin the journey back to her room, her demand was to be picked up. Holding her hand was too easy. She didn't want to be led; she wanted to be carried through the dark place. She would look at me with half-opened eyes, filled with tears, stretch her hands as far as they could reach, and scream, "Daddy, pick me up!" She had already learned this life lesson: Daddy is not going to let her cry long, and when she needs me to, I'll pick her up.

Whether we like it or not, each of us experiences "night seasons" in our lives. No one is exempt, and everyone must be willing to go through them. Truth be told, many of us would agree that we have stubbed our toes, ran into walls, and experienced all types of foolishness in the midst of these dark times. If we were to be even more honest, we would admit that those times were the loneliest and most challenging of our lives. Night seasons are never fun, but when we walk through them, they always strengthen our relationship with the Father.

There are so many words of affirmation the Bible gives us pertaining to God's consistency in being with us in the most challenging seasons of our lives. It may seem as if we are on our own at times, but our greatest assurance is that the presence of God is ever with us, ready and willing to pick us up whenever we need Him. Our faith rests in the fact that the

Lord is the Lifter of our Heads. He will not only pick us up when life becomes overwhelming and challenging, but He will also allow us to remain focused on our future.

Just as Londyn learned this lesson, so should we. The Lord will pick us up. As believers, we are granted certain guarantees. We are children of the King. We belong to the Father. We are heirs of God and joint-heirs with Christ. For the sake of our relationship, God won't allow us to stay down long if we are ready to get back up. Situations in life may throw us off temporarily, but our reassurance is in the fact that the Father will not allow us to be utterly cast down. He has invested in our success through the sacrifice of His Son, Jesus Christ.

Today, I want you to be reminded that your Father is always on night duty. No matter how dark or desperate the place, if you call on Him, He will pick you up and carry you through your challenges. He knows and understands your tears and your hurt. Despite what you may feel, He is ready to pick you up and carry you through your storms!

Don't despise the night seasons of your life! Allow them to be a tool for God to demonstrate His incredible faithfulness to you!

PURPOSE PRAYER

Heavenly Father,

There are so many days when I know I simply need to be picked up and carried through the circumstances that I'm facing. There are times I find myself in a whirlwind of challenges wondering when my Help is coming. But today, I take full confidence in the fact that in every situation, You are well able to pick me up! I lift my eyes to You!

I declare that my night seasons will not keep me from running to You, my Help. I declare that the darkest hour of my situations is preparing me for the daybreak that is about to dawn in my life. And most importantly, I declare that I trust You to carry me through it all.

In Jesus' Name, Amen.

PURPOSE FOCUS

What have you been trying to walk yourself through without the counsel of God?

When was the last time you allowed God to pick you up without neglecting the way He was doing it?

Have you been able to see how your night seasons have benefitted your purpose?

23

Following the Right Steps

MORNING MEDITATION

Psalm 37:23-26, New International Version

The Lord makes firm the steps of the one who delights in him; though he may stumble, he will not fall, for the Lord upholds him with his hand. I was young and now I am old, yet I have never seen the righteous forsaken or their children begging bread. They are always generous and lend freely; their children will be a blessing.

EVENING DEVOTION

Psalm 119:129-133, New International Version

Your decrees are wonderful; therefore my soul keeps them. The unfolding of your words gives light; it imparts understanding to the simple. With open mouth I pant, because I long for your commandments. Turn to me and be gracious to me, as is your custom toward those who love your name. Keep my steps steady according to your promise, and never let iniquity have dominion over me.

Tulsa, Oklahoma is the place my family will always consider home. It was the first place we lived together, where the first doors of full-time ministry were opened, and also the place where we learned how to walk in the footsteps God selected for our lives. This understanding did not always come with ease, yet through each lesson, we could always see the hand of God, and that kept us in the right place.

One evening while grocery shopping with Ashriel, she decided she didn't want to ride in the cart. Instead, she wanted to walk like a big girl. The walk started out like most with Ashriel running randomly around the store to every aisle that suited her fancy. Finally, I told her that if she wanted to be free, then she needed to walk with Daddy. At that mild rebuke, she immediately straightened up and started walking behind me. When I asked her why she was walking behind me, her response was pure and innocent: "Daddy, I just want to walk in the same steps you take."

Before you ever came into the world, the Lord knew you by name and custom-designed the steps you should take in life. He knew what your strengths would be. He understood from where your weaknesses would come. He knew the things that would make you "tick" and the things that would make you want to tuck tail and run. In every situation, He has ordered your steps so that you could follow the path He prescribed for your life. The only thing left for you to do is to follow the prescribed steps.

The power of walking in God's purpose is that you are in sync with His ordered steps for your life. When we recognize that God has a specific plan for us, we should seek to walk in those steps every day of our lives. Being in sync with God's steps has nothing to do with religious formalities and everything to do with forging a sensitive relationship with God. This relationship will enable you to be sensitive to His will for your life and eventually, see that will become a reality.

No matter how hard Ashriel tried, she could never completely fill my shoes or take each step I took, yet she never quit trying. We have the ability to walk out the God-ordained steps for our lives. The grace for us is that even when we take the wrong steps, God will correct us and place us back on the right path when we remain open and synchronize our hearts to His.

The Lord has watched every step that you have ever taken in your life. He knows where you have been and more importantly, He knows where you are going! The plan that God ordered for your life is custom-made. It will not look like anyone else's because it was designed specifically for you. Today, allow your relationship with God take on new value based on the fact that His great love for you caused Him to create a specific destiny for your life. Your future is so bright and full of hope because of God's plan for you. Do not allow yourself to become bogged down thinking about what you have not done or could not do. Time will be wasted if you spend it comparing yourself to anyone else. Focus only on what God designed for you to do!

So your steps have gotten out of line once or twice? Join the crowd. Discovering God's path for you is a journey riddled with trial and error. As you grow in the knowledge of God, focus less on your wrong steps and more on learning to walk in the rhythm of God's will for your life. Learn that as you synchronize your steps with His, He will continue to lead you down the surest path of growth and prosperity for every area of your life.

PURPOSE PRAYER

Heavenly Father,

I want to walk down the path You have designed for my life. I want the custom-made destiny that can only be unlocked by walking in the steps You have ordered for my life. Today, I will accept no more detours–I only want Your design for my life. I believe that as I walk in Your will, You will delight in every step that I take. My steps no longer belong to me–each step belongs to You.

I declare that my steps are in sync with Your purpose for my life. I declare that You keep my steps are in alignment with Your plans. I declare that my steps will not be guided by distractions, but by my call to destiny. I declare that this is my day and my moment to walk in Your authority and power and I fully embrace it. I am taking the right steps.

In Jesus' Name, Amen.

PURPOSE FOCUS

Do you trust God and the steps that He has ordered for your purpose? How has your life reflected that?

How have you watched your life get out of sync with His will? How did you re-align it?

What have you had to walk away from to walk closer to Him? Was it worth it?

24

Let It Go

MORNING MEDITATION

Psalm 86:5-7, New International Version

You, Lord, are forgiving and good, abounding in love to all who call to you. Hear my prayer, LORD; listen to my cry for mercy. When I am in distress, I call to you, because you answer me.

EVENING DEVOTION

Matthew 6:14-15, New International Version

For if you forgive other people when they sin against you, your heavenly Father will also forgive you. But if you do not forgive others their sins, your Father will not forgive your sins.

One of the most powerful things we experienced as a family was when the girls learned to forgive each other. Any given week, there may be a number of altercations between the oldest three. We've watched them get mad at each other, and it lasts anywhere from five seconds to the next day. What we love is that every time, without question, they find a way to forgive each other and move on with their little lives.

However, there is a difference between simply asking for forgiveness and truly giving a heartfelt apology. Such is the case with Amana who has become infamous for her pseudo-apologies given in the heat of the moment so she can embark on her next adventure as soon as possible. She's mastered the art of saying she's sorry, all the while plotting her next opportunity to strike at one of her unsuspecting sisters.

One particular afternoon, Amana was terrorizing Londyn over their toys. The moment Londyn began playing with one, Amana would come up behind her, take it, and scream, "Mine!" This quickly escalated from just taking Londyn's toys to pulling the bows out of her hair. The moment the first bow left Londyn's hair, little feet flew to our room to tell us what had happened. Before she could get the words out good, Amana came up quickly behind yelling, "Sorry!"

This pattern went on until Amana snatched about three or four bows from Londyn's hair. At that point, I sent Amana to her room to think about what she'd done. Within five minutes, Amana came back to us in tears, pleading with her eyes saying "Sorry!" over and over. But this time, it was different. When Amana apologized, Londyn was not having it. She was furious over the removal of her hair bows even though Phineka had already put them back. She did not want to forgive Amana.

This went on for days. They played together, but the moment Amana did the smallest thing Londyn didn't like, she reminded her of what had happened just days before. She even went so far as to threaten to tell on Amana again for the same thing.

After a week of this, we finally told Londyn it was time to let it go. It didn't make any sense to tattle about what had happened days before. It was over. If she had truly forgiven Amana, then it was time to stop bringing up old stuff. After a few moments, what we said finally sunk in. It didn't happen instantaneously, but once Londyn released it, she never brought it up again.

The concept of releasing and letting a thing go is a tough one to swallow, yet it is so important! We cannot control everything that happens to us, but we can control whether or not we choose to let something go. So often, we lose time, energy, focus, and purpose, all because we refuse to forgive and move on with our lives. Whatever we hold on to will keep us from moving forward in God's purpose for our lives.

Unforgiveness is like a disease that eats away at us from the inside out. Oftentimes, people don't know what we are dealing with because we don't open up and release the toxins of hurt and pain from our past. Therefore, we slowly erode and wither away inside. What we choose to hold on to typically has a better hold on us than we have on it.

No one wants to walk around bound for life. It would be a sad, unfulfilling life to behold a world of possibilities, yet be too bound to experience it. This is exactly what happens when we allow unforgiveness to rule our lives. We are handcuffed to situations that are no longer worth our time. More often than not, the people we need to forgive have moved on with their lives while we remain bound in the past. There is freedom in letting go. There is freedom to move forward, walk in liberty, be released, and be restored. God calls us to forgive and move forward in our lives for a reason: He did not design us to be bound. When you release the things that have choked the life out of you, you will have a renewed sense of purpose, passion for living, and pursuit of everything that God destined for your life.

Today, take the time to examine your heart and discover if you are harboring any unforgiveness. The quicker you remove unforgiveness, the less likely you are to deal with its consequences such as anger, bitterness, etc. Though it may be challenging to deal with, make this your day to let go. Forget about what happened and embrace what will happen when you choose to walk forward in the purpose of God!

PURPOSE PRAYER

Heavenly Father,

I do not want to harbor feelings, emotions, or ideas that add to my frustration and rob me of my future. I want to identify people, things, and situations that have broken my heart, injured my spirit, and caused me to doubt who I am in God. I want to release offenses and not look for them. Today, I choose to let go.

I declare that the pain of my past is not worth holding on to. I declare that I forgive because I have been forgiven. I declare that even through the pain of release, You restore my heart, my mind, and my spirit. I declare that what I have experienced is a testimony of the restorative power of God. I declare that even though I have been broken, I am healed now!

In Jesus' name, Amen.

PURPOSE FOCUS

Who/what keeps reminding you of who you use to be?

How has this reminder impeded you of your pursuit of purpose?

Have you let yourself go and forgiven your missteps so that you could fully embrace His ordered plan for your life?

25

Living in Purpose

MORNING MEDITATION

Proverbs 19:21, New International Version

Many are the plans in a person's heart, but it is the LORD's purpose that prevails.

EVENING DEVOTION

Philippians 1:3-6, New International Version

I thank my God every time I remember you. In all my prayers for all of you, I always pray with joy because of your partnership in the gospel from the first day until now, being confident of this, that he who began a good work in you will carry it on to completion until the day of Christ Jesus.

Since Ashriel is our oldest daughter, we have been able to watch her personality and purpose evolve much longer than the other three. Since she was a small girl, we have watched her love and care for others with a great concern for almost anyone who crosses her path. Her heart to express God's heart through serving others was evident as early as three-years-old and kept Phineka and I watching her growth with awe and appreciation to God for who she is.

These traits became increasingly evident even as we prepared for Ashriel's eighth birthday. We agreed that we would throw a party for her as we typically do for birthdays. We allowed her to select the friends from her class as well as church that would participate. All of the plans were made to have her party on a Thursday, the actual weekday of her birth.

The day before the party, Ashriel realized that she had a "schedule conflict." Every Thursday, she works with one of our church ministries feeding and caring for the homeless. We noticed the conflict as we were planning the party but just assumed that she chose to have her party instead of serving the homeless on this particular occasion.

When we sat down to discuss the conflict the morning of her birthday, Ashriel made a bold declaration. Her paraphrased resolution was this:

"Dad, serving the homeless is my ministry. If I cannot go serve them, I do not want to have a party. They are expecting me, and I would rather be there."

As I drove her to school that morning with "mist" in my eyes, I realized that at eight-years-old, my baby was beginning to tap into one of the most crucial aspects of her life–discovering the value of purpose and pouring her life out in service to others.

We know that we have truly begun the journey towards purpose when we want to do what we are passionate about even if no one pays us for it. You see, all of us have something placed inside of us since before the beginning time by God that we are destined to fulfill–our purpose. It is the essence of why our Father created us. Without purpose, our lives are pointless.

With that in mind, we all have to continuously walk the journey of discovery that allows us to peel back the layers that reveal the reason for our existence. We cannot be purpose-driven and satisfied with mundane living at the same time. We must strive daily to walk in God's purpose for our existence. Destiny is not a destination. It's a continuous journey on the road to fulfilling God's plan for our lives.

We know that we are living in purpose when there is nothing else we would rather do. We wholeheartedly give ourselves to fulfilling it. We want to give it our best at all times and in all ways. We are bold enough to give up our wants and desires to serve that purpose to the best of our abilities. When purpose is found, it must be continuously pursued.

Furthermore, our purpose and passions often come into perfect alignment with each other. When we become a new creation and align our lives with Christ, our passions should come into alignment as well. It is out of that passion that God directs us toward fulfilling His purpose for our lives. There are many who ask, "What is my purpose?" The response for me is simple: "What is your passion?" Once you tap into one, the other is soon revealed.

Greater than simply walking in purpose, God created all of us to be servants to each other. To serve one another is a concept that is becoming extinct in our society and among generations as a whole. In a nutshell, to be servants or serve others means that you prefer others over yourself. It means that you are humble enough to place your desires in the backseat to facilitate someone else's needs. When we serve people out of a pure heart as Christ did, we will not only see the lives of others change, but our lives will change as well.

Today, spend time reexamining your purpose for living. Engage God with challenging questions pertaining to your life by simply asking, "Why?" Allow your spirit to be sensitive to the Holy Spirit as He begins to reveal things and possibly even redirect the steps to your life so that you can fulfill your purpose for living. Even when it does not seem like it or feel like it, I assure you, you were created on purpose to live in purpose. Embrace all that the Father has for your life!

PURPOSE PRAYER

Heavenly Father,

I know that I was created with purpose. I am not an accident, but a part of Your awesome handiwork. You understand me better than anyone else ever could. I believe in the power of purpose and know that there is a destiny for me to fulfill in the earth. I am committed to You and to myself to fulfill Your plan for my life.

I declare that nothing will stop me from walking in the purpose You designed for me. I declare that every mountain that has attempted to impede my progress is rubble beneath my feet. I declare that I pour out my life like oil in service to You and others and that the world will know I am Yours by the unconditional love I display to them. I declare that I am driven by purpose and Your plan for my life!

In Jesus' Name, Amen.

PURPOSE FOCUS

What has caused you to fear God's purpose for your life?

For you, what does walking in purpose look like? How will that be achieved for this next season of your life?

What can others see in you that you refuse to recognize in your own self?

Pushing Through the Pain

26

MORNING MEDITATION

Psalm 30:1-5, New International Version

I will exalt you, Lord, for you lifted me out of the depths and did not let my enemies gloat over me. Lord my God, I called to you for help, and you healed me. You, Lord, brought me up from the realm of the dead; you spared me from going down to the pit. Sing the praises of the Lord, you his faithful people; praise his holy name. For his anger lasts only a moment, but his favor lasts a lifetime; weeping may stay for the night, but rejoicing comes in the morning.

EVENING DEVOTION

II Corinthians 4:16-18, New International Version

Therefore we do not lose heart. Though outwardly we are wasting away, yet inwardly we are being renewed day by day. For our light and momentary troubles are achieving for us an eternal glory that far outweighs them all. So we fix our eyes not on what is seen, but on what is unseen, since what is seen is temporary, but what is unseen is eternal.

On November 18th, 2010, Phineka and I were blessed to welcome our third daughter, Amana Leigh, into the world. This pregnancy was vastly different from the others. For starters, we WERE NOT expecting a child in that season of our lives. We had Londyn almost (exactly) one year before, and we were in the midst of settling into a new life in Chattanooga, TN with no expectation of a family expansion. We were overwhelmed to be entrusted with the phenomenal responsibility of bringing another daughter into the world.

I still remember the evening of the delivery as if it were a moment ago. We raced to the emergency room and experienced dilation within an hour of arrival. After getting Phineka prepped for delivery, they discovered it was all progressing so quickly that they would not have time to give her an epidural. I was overwhelmed with emotion as I watched her lay helplessly on the hospital bed, enduring the pain of each contraction.

When the doctor came into the room and prepared for delivery, I looked into my wife's eyes and she told me she didn't think she could do it. Now, you have to understand, I am married to one of the strongest women to ever walk the face of the earth. Her tolerance for pain is supernatural, but it seemed that she would not be able to endure the pain of this delivery. At that moment, the doctor looked at her and said one thing, "Push through the pain."

He promised her that if she could push past the temporary feeling of pain, that she would receive something she had been waiting on for nine months. I watched my wife tearfully bear down and push as hard as she could. Moments later, we heard the first cry of our "miracle baby."

Phineka's experience sums up that of many others. One of the most challenging things to do in life is to focus beyond the pain of the present to attain the reward on the other side. It is all the more challenging when people have given up on us, written us off, attempt to speak death over our lives, and so on.

Today, you may be sitting in a place where you are one push away from releasing the greatness within you, yet the pain of the moment has created a temporary paralysis in your desire to move forward. Pain has a paralyzing tendency that can only be conquered by your desire to overcome! No one can deny the pain is real, yet the greater reality is that if you push past the moment, what you release will triumph over what you experienced! Do not spend another moment of your life paralyzed by the pain of producing greatness–you were created to push past this. Push through the pain!

A good portion of life is spent dealing with pain. Thank God, His Word contains promises that remind us that the pain produces something greater in our lives. Weeping and pain are temporary, while the joy of overcoming is greater than the possibility of failure. Regardless of people's opinions, you can and you will make it through this. As a matter of fact, what you are experiencing is only a light affliction in the grand scheme of things. With that in mind, know that God is working out something great as we boldly endure our circumstances. Pain is temporary, but joy endures forever.

What pain have you experienced that is causing you to doubt the greatness for which God designed you? What has caused the deterioration of the lens through which you view life? The pain of the experience cannot be wiped away, but know this–you can push past the pain! The feeling of discomfort need not prevail in your life. Today is the day that you give life one more mighty push and expect great things to come!

PURPOSE PRAYER

Heavenly Father,

Today, my pain will motivate me to press onward. It may not feel good at the moment, but I trust and believe that it is working for my good. Lord, give me the strength and resolve to conquer the most painful circumstances. Give me the steadfastness to keep going even in the midst of adversity.

I declare that my night seasons are the right seasons for me to birth my purpose in You. I declare that the pain of moving forward will not stop me from progressing in Your will for my life. I may have been hurt in one area or another in life, but I declare that pain will not prevent me from moving forward. I declare that I am pushing through the pain!

In Jesus' Name, Amen.

PURPOSE FOCUS

Have you ever been paralyzed while pursuing purpose? What finally jolted you from your place of pain?

How fearful has your life been of what may not work out? Has that ever stopped you from moving forward into all that God designed for you?

Have you learned how to press through difficulties? What is the hardest thing you have ever pressed through? How did it end up?

You've Outgrown This

27

MORNING DEVOTION

II Peter 3:17-18, New Revised Standard Version

You therefore, beloved, since you are forewarned, beware that you are not carried away with the error of the lawless and lose your own stability. But grow in the grace and knowledge of our Lord and Savior Jesus Christ. To him be the glory both now and to the day of eternity. Amen.

EVENING DEVOTION

Philippians 1:4-6, New Revised Standard Version

I thank my God every time I remember you, constantly praying with joy in every one of my prayers for all of you, because of your sharing in the gospel from the first day until now. I am confident of this, that the one who began a good work among you will bring it to completion by the day of Jesus Christ.

It was quite a journey watching Amana grow into a toddler. As she made her transitions, they didn't always come without their share of knocks and bruises. One of her favorite games to play to keep away from her sisters was running under the kitchen table. She knew that she could run under quickly, but they would have to stop and duck in order to avoid getting hurt in the process.

One spring afternoon, Amana went about the game as she typically did, but something unexpected happened. She bumped her head–and hard! After crying for several minutes, she went back to playing. The next time she came to the table, she stopped, looked, and ducked so she could get under it. She remembered the pain of hitting her head before and, in her own small way, realized that she had outgrown her ability to do what used to work for her.

How often do we, like Amana, find ourselves still attempting to do things that we've outgrown? With each attempt, we find ourselves bumping our heads over and over again. Time management, relationships, finances, etc., the list goes on. We know that there has to be a less challenging way to go about things, but the proverbial knots on our head tell a different story.

If we believe that God is continually working to fulfill His purpose in our lives, then we must be continually growing and maturing in our personal walk with Him. We can never become stagnant or accustomed to the status quo. We must be willing to push the limits daily and exceed our expectations for life and purpose. Anything that isn't growing is dying. We can never become so satisfied with where we are that we no longer attempt to accomplish the next feat God has for us.

We must all be willing to go through transition. With each progression, we understand that certain things will no longer be present. If you've found yourself going through the same struggles year after year, that means God is trying to mature you, but you refuse to accept it and are thus doomed to go through the same cycle over and over until you learn your lesson. You must accept the challenge of looking at yourself as well as your situation and be honest enough to say enough is enough. You cannot go where you refuse to grow.

Growth is a process that often comes with pain, hence the term "growing pains." However, the pain of growth should not stop you from progressing. When we were children, we did childish things. However, when we grow, our actions must represent that growth. Can you imagine wearing a bib to meals as a full-grown adult? The bib was fine when you were an infant, but now you don't need it. As we grow in our relationship with God, He'll begin to wean us off of the things we've outgrown. Not because those things are necessarily bad, but because they're no longer necessary.

What do you find yourself returning to even after God has pulled you away from it? What are the secret temptations that continually seduce you away from God? What are the things that are not even technically a sin, but draw you away from God by occupying your time and thoughts? There must be a time when you admit, "I've outgrown this!"

Take this day to assess the habits you've outgrown. It could be as simple as the time you spend watching television or playing video games, addictions you've had since childhood, and so forth and so on. For every habit you break, fill the void with a renewed focus on growing your relationship with God as well as bettering yourself. As you continue to mature in Him, you'll find that you've actually outgrown many things. Don't shrink back to old habits! Choose to grow up!

PURPOSE PRAYER

Heavenly Father,

I know there are things in my life that I have outgrown. Today, I ask that You would help me leave behind the old habits, ideas, and even people that seek to hinder my progress in You. I don't want to box myself into who I was, but grow into the person You've called me to be. I choose to leave the old me behind and grow into the child of God You have called me to be!

I declare that childish things have passed away and that I am the full measure of a person living in purpose. I declare that God has started a good work in my life and that He will see it through to completion. I declare that I will not shrink back into things that I have outgrown, but will stand with the full assurance of who You have called me to be.

In Jesus' Name, Amen.

PURPOSE FOCUS

What have you outgrown that you are still trying to fit into? How is what you are trying to force impeding your purpose?

Are you ok with being despised by those you have outgrown?

What childish things is God still calling you to put away?

28

The Trust Factor

MORNING MEDITATION

Psalm 20:6-8, New Revised Standard Version

Now I know that the Lord will help his anointed; he will answer him from his holy heaven with mighty victories by his right hand. Some take pride in chariots, and some in horses, but our pride is in the name of the Lord our God. They will collapse and fall, but we shall rise and stand upright.

EVENING DEVOTION

Psalm 18:1-3, New Revised Standard Version

I love you, O Lord, my strength. The Lord is my rock, my fortress, and my deliverer, my God, my rock in whom I take refuge, my shield, and the horn of my salvation, my stronghold. I call upon the Lord, who is worthy to be praised, so I shall be saved from my enemies.

Children are daredevils. Full-grown adults are often in shock over some of the things children try. At such a young age, they seem to be ingrained with fearlessness. Some say that their adventurous nature comes from naïveté of potential dangers. Others say it is their childlike faith that causes them to test every man-made boundary in life. Whatever the reason, this "dare-devilishness" is a stark reality in our home.

As a toddler, Amana had a favorite game she loved to play. This game remained nameless in our home because we had continuously tried to talk her out of it, yet it remained her favorite thing to do. She would take her little body, climb atop the couch, look at her mother or me, and simply says one word: "hand!" When she said that, we knew what would inevitably follow. After grasping the extended hand, she would lean her tiny frame off the edge of the couch to the point where it seemed as if she'd fall. She had learned that as long as she was holding the right hand, she never had to worry about falling. You see, she never asked one of her sisters to hold her hand in this game. Even at a young age, Amana understood that the success of her game relied entirely on the hand she held.

Life often places us in predicaments where our victory is rooted in our faith that God will hold us in the midst of our circumstances. If we are honest with ourselves, I believe we would all admit that at least once or twice in our lives, we fell flat on our faces because our trust was placed in the wrong things. We trust our finances more than we trust the faithful provision of God. We trust shaky relationships more than we trust the constancy of God. The list could go on, yet the result would be the same. Our trust must be firmly rooted in God if we expect to experience continued success in our lives.

Flaky faith always produces flaky results. In every area of our lives, we must believe God more than we believe our capacity to error. We cannot have a fair-weather faith. We must trust God no matter the circumstance. We must trust Him no matter what challenges may come our way.

Complete faith in God is not a matter of knowing the next step, but of knowing that as you take that step, you are holding onto the right Hand. Most things in life are not perfect or predictable, but we know that we can always strive to trust God more tomorrow than we did today. We may not know what tomorrow holds, but we know Who holds it. As we continue to stretch our faith in God, He will continue to show us His unconditional love and divine guidance in every facet of our lives.

Today, take your faith in God to the next level. Trust Him like never before. Take a leap of faith and know that He will catch you mid-flight. Release yourself from the limitations of man-made hope and uncover the fullness of greatness that God has in store for you through faith. Hold onto God's hand and take a chance that will change your life!

PURPOSE PRAYER

Heavenly Father,

I cast down every thought and every imagination that has ever caused me to doubt You. Please forgive me for trusting myself more than You. Help me to know that as I hold to Your unchanging hand and trust You, You will lead me down the paths that will cause me to grow in You. I give You my whole heart and know that as I do, I am being conformed to your perfect will for my life.

I declare that my faith is being increased as I pray this prayer. I declare that my faith will not be in horses or chariots, but in the name of the Lord. I declare that You are my Rock and Fortress and that Your name is the Refuge for my life. I declare that even in the face of insurmountable obstacles, I trust You.

In Jesus' Name, Amen.

PURPOSE FOCUS

Who do you trust the most? How have they earned that trust in your life?

How have you been flaky in your faith? Has that held up what God was trying to do in your heart and life?

Has the fear of falling kept you from grasping the right hand? Who is your destiny holding on to?

29

The Search

MORNING MEDITATION

I Corinthians 2:9-13, New International Version

However, as it is written: "What no eye has seen, what no ear has heard, and what no human mind has conceived"–the things God has prepared for those who love him– these are the things God has revealed to us by his Spirit. The Spirit searches all things, even the deep things of God. For who knows a person's thoughts except their own spirit within them? In the same way no one knows the thoughts of God except the Spirit of God. What we have received is not the spirit of the world, but the Spirit who is from God, so that we may understand what God has freely given us. This is what we speak, not in words taught us by human wisdom but in words taught by the Spirit, explaining spiritual realities with Spirit-taught words.

EVENING DEVOTION

Psalm 119:114-117, New International Version

You are my refuge and my shield; I have put my hope in your word. Away from me, you evildoers, that I may keep the commands of my God! Sustain me, my God, according to your promise, and I will live; do not let my hopes be dashed. Uphold me, and I will be delivered; I will always have regard for your decrees.

When Phineka and I discovered we were pregnant with Layel, we determined that was it. We had tried for a son, and it didn't happen. We were more than pleased with the fact that God entrusted us with four daughters. This resolution also became a reality because Phineka determined that she had done her duty to "be fruitful and multiply." We fulfilled our responsibility and were satisfied with our contribution to the world!

Although we had made this resolution together, others around us–including our daughters–did not know it. One evening within a few weeks of Layel coming home from the hospital, our daughters all came into our room and climbed into the bed with us. Ashriel served as the spokeswoman for the trio. Her serious look coupled with the giggles of the other two let us know that something was up.

"We still want a brother!" The girls had commenced this impromptu family meeting to present their petition for a brother. "We were talking, and we think that we should have one more baby. When do you think we can get one?" The look of bewilderment on Phineka's face spoke almost as loudly as the girls' request. Before she could respond, I let the girls know that Layel was our final addition and that we were grateful to God for what He had blessed us with.

"Are you sure? Because we REALLY want a brother." At this last remark, Phineka swiftly responded, "This is it! Now go to bed." That set off a symphony of laughter and entertainment for the girls. As they marched away to their rooms, Londyn looked back for one final confirmation and said, "So, that means no brother?"

Since we resolved that our baby-making days had come to an end, it was not hard for us to deny the requests or pressure that came from any outside influence. Our resolution was firm. Our minds were set. We knew what God had spoken to us concerning our family, and we were sticking to it no matter what.

Our focus on our purpose must have this same level of resolve and assurance when it comes to walking out the call of God on our lives. It is always amazing how people attempt to persuade you of what is best for your life when you have already consulted God, heard His voice clearly, and understand your Kingdom mandates. There must be a resolve in our hearts that no matter what people try to put on us, we will only want what God wants.

Pressure cannot push us away from our purpose. I have discovered that pressure comes in many forms and wears many faces. There will be pressure from family and loved ones who have your best interests in mind, yet may not have the mind of God for you in this season of life. There will be pressure from your circles of influence to see you walk in your destiny. There will also be pressure from those who oppose you and simply want to see you fall. Whatever direction the pressure comes from, you must be willing to stand firm on what God has for you!

Our daughters' request to give them a brother did not mean they loved us any less. They just had an agenda that they wanted to see become a reality in our lives. Do not allow the agenda of others to alter God's agenda for your life. You have a God-breathed, God-crafted purpose that you must fulfill. Once you tap into His will for your life, you cannot deny what He has destined for you!

There is a major difference between a good thing and a God thing. You can do a lot of good stuff, but if that good stuff does not equate to God's will, you have simply wasted your time. Once you discover God's plan and path for your life, your focus must be like that of an eagle. You must hone in on what is for you and remove everything else from your vision.

Today, ask God for His mind regarding your purpose and resolve not to settle for anything less than His perfect will. Will questions come internally and externally? Yes, without a shadow of a doubt. However, when you know what God has said, every other question quickly fades into the background. Let this begin the process of weighing every question and decision against God's purpose for you. If it doesn't fit into God's purpose, refuse to make it your focus!

PURPOSE PRAYER

Heavenly Father,

I want nothing less than what You have destined and designed for my life. I do not want to take on tasks, responsibilities, and opportunities that cause me to busy myself with the wrong thing in the wrong season. Today, I pray for the focus that comes from the Your Spirit, which gives me the boldness to say "no" when necessary, and to only accept what is in line with my life's purpose.

I declare that I will not be bogged down with distractions from my purpose. I declare that everything seeking to steal my focus, occupy my thoughts, and bankrupt my emotions is null and void in the name of Jesus. I declare that I will see the fullness of what God has created for me and that I walk by the Spirit to receive everything pertaining to my life and destiny. I declare that I will receive all that God has for me-nothing more and nothing less. This is it!

In Jesus' Name, Amen.

PURPOSE FOCUS

Have you ever succumbed to pressure from people to perform? How did that alter the way you felt about who you were?

Have you created healthy boundaries by which you act and respond to those who try to force your life in a different direction than God designed?

Who do you trust to keep you accountable to fulfilling what God placed in your hands?

30

You Are a Survivor

MORNING MEDITATION

Romans 8:28-31, New Revised Standard Version

We know that all things work together for good for those who love God, who are called according to his purpose. For those whom he foreknew he also predestined to be conformed to the image of his Son, in order that he might be the firstborn within a large family. And those whom he predestined he also called; and those whom he called he also justified; and those whom he justified he also glorified. What then are we to say about these things? If God is for us, who is against us?

EVENING DEVOTION

Psalm 36:7-10, New Revised Standard Version

How precious is your steadfast love, O God! All people may take refuge in the shadow of your wings. They feast on the abundance of your house, and you give them drink from the river of your delights. For with you is the fountain of life; in your light we see light. O continue your steadfast love to those who know you, and your salvation to the upright of heart!

April 5, 2010 is a date that will forever be etched in my brain. We were living in Chattanooga, TN with Ashriel and our then newborn, Londyn. We had just discovered that Phineka was pregnant again and we were early in the first trimester. We sat watching the final game of the NCAA Basketball Tournament when Phineka stood up to get something to drink from the kitchen. That was when we looked up and saw the trail of blood following her.

We were all too familiar with this scenario. We had miscarried once before and knew that this was one of the signs. We left the girls with my mom and rushed Phineka to the emergency room. After what seemed like hours of testing, the prognosis they brought back was a grim one. The baby had detached itself from the safe place along Phineka's fallopian tubes, and a miscarriage was imminent. I remember us attempting to console one another while at the same time rejecting the doctor's diagnosis.

A few weeks later, we went back for a follow-up. Since the doctors knew what had transpired, their expectation was to find nothing in the x-rays. As the nurse began the ultrasound, she stopped about halfway through and went to get the doctor. Much to their surprise, the womb they thought was empty had a growing baby inside! Though they could not understand the baby's survival, we knew one thing for certain–God was allowing us to bring a survivor into the world.

As you reflect on your life, your situation may have been completely different surrounding your entrance into the world. Nevertheless, life has a way of dealing blows that make us all wonder how we survived them. The answer is not at all complex–you are a survivor! God created you with a purpose, and you cannot die until it is fulfilled in the earth! Nothing can destroy what God created to live. Since He alone is the Giver of Life and Releaser of Purpose, who He brings into existence is entirely intentional. You may have felt you didn't have a purpose at one point or another, but the truth of the matter is that God does not make mistakes. If He placed you here, then there is a purpose for your life.

Before Amana ever came into the world, she confused human logic and confounded reason all because of purpose. God did not wait for the permission of people to create you and your purpose. What He ordained for your life from your mother's womb must come into existence. God will never take back His purpose for your life. He simply wants you to walk in it.

As you reflect on your life, I am sure you can remember challenges, circumstances, and even life-altering experiences that others did not survive. I am sure you can remember instances where your life has literally flashed before you. There is probably at least one time you can recollect in which you should have died, but you didn't. Why? Because God's purpose is stronger than any force working against His will for your life. When we choose to follow Him, He chooses to reveal His purpose for our lives. Your resolve must be that since God gave you life, you are going to live it for His glory, allowing Him to completely lead you into the fulfillment of your purpose. Every day will not be a bed of roses, yet you cannot settle for living a mediocre life filled with frustration and disgust caused by the lack of purpose. There is a clear call from God on your life, and you will never be satisfied until it is filled.

Even in your most frustrating moments, it only takes a moment to reflect on the fact that you are a survivor. God did not allow you to live so that you could waste your life. He did it so you could live in His glory and show others the way to Him. Once you realize that you survived what others have not, pursuing God should never get tiring or frustrating.

Today, think about your own story and experiences. Reflect on from where God has brought you. Focus on why He allowed you to make it out. When you weigh it all–the good, the bad, the ugly, and indifferent–you will see that God is for you! He used it all to work together for your good. You are His handiwork, the crown jewel of His creation. Do not allow your life to be wasted pursuing temporary pleasures. God allowed you to survive to finish the story for which you were created. Believe it or not, you are a survivor!

PURPOSE PRAYER

Heavenly Father,

Thank you for preserving my life. Others died going through what I survived. I know for sure that there is a plan for my life and I will not be satisfied until that purpose is revealed for all the world to see. I am purpose-driven because I survived and thrive in life.

I declare that my experiences will not be wasted. I declare that my life's purpose will manifest for all to see. I declare that I survived and will continue to survive until my life is completely poured out for Your glory. I declare that all things work out for my good because I love You and am called according to Your purpose. I declare that I am a survivor!

In Jesus' Name, Amen.

PURPOSE FOCUS

What is the thing that you have survived that you know was only by the hand of God?

How has that become a positive reflection on your purpose and destiny?

How will your story bless and change the lives of countless others?

31

Praying for Purpose

MORNING MEDITATION

Psalm 37:3-6, New International Version

Trust in the LORD and do good; dwell in the land and enjoy safe pasture. Take delight in the LORD, and he will give you the desires of your heart. Commit your way to the LORD; trust in him and he will do this: He will make your righteous reward shine like the dawn, your vindication like the noonday sun.

EVENING DEVOTION

Ephesians 2:8-10, New International Version

For it is by grace you have been saved, through faith—and this is not from yourselves, it is the gift of God—not by works, so that no one can boast. For we are God's handiwork, created in Christ Jesus to do good works, which God prepared in advance for us to do.

One of my favorite times of the day is right before bedtime with the girls. As we finish unwinding from the day, we all sit in a circle on the floor and have our prayer time. Though my schedule varies from week to week based on the demands of my job, this is the part of my family time that I treasure most. When the girls connect with God through prayer in their special way, it keeps my prayers over them for their respective purposes all the more pressing on my heart.

On a typical night, Amana will lead a song of her choosing before we pray. Once the song is over, they go around in the circle from oldest to youngest praying for whatever comes into their head. Sometimes it will be simple prayers of thanksgiving for everything that transpired in the day. Other times, they pray for God to bless and cover our family and all of the families around the world. The simplicity of the prayers based on their respective ages and personalities are a pure expression of their heart for God.

Once finished, they all will scoot toward Phineka and me. They know that every time we pray together, we will lay our hands on their heads and pray for peaceful rest and for God's purpose to be continually revealed in their lives. They smile in anticipation of the words of affirmation and blessing spoken over their lives before bedtime. Even if they do not yet fully understand it, purpose-filled prayers for them to become all that God destined them to be are continually released over their lives.

Throughout this devotional, I pray your faith has been stretched, your walk has been challenged, and your purpose has become all the more real in your life. Though every aspect of it may not be crystal clear at present, my prayer is that you have come to a place where you feel yourself walking closer with God than when you began.

Keep praying for purpose. As you pray for God to continually reveal His will for your life, pray that His purpose will become a reality that you live out every second of every minute of every hour of every day. Destiny is not a one-stop location; it is a continual journey as we evolve into the people God created us to be.

As you pray for the revelation of your purpose, continue to pray for those with whom you are connected. Ask God to show them His wisdom in creating them, His purpose in maintaining them, as well as His plan for their lives. When we pray for the purpose of others, we are essentially fulfilling one of the main purposes in our own lives–that all would discover the will of God for their lives.

You may be at a crossroad in your life that has you questioning what God will do next. Even in the silent seasons of your life, God is yet giving direction. We must all learn to trust Him even when it seems that His responses to our prayers are non-existent. Keep praying and pushing for your purpose even when it seems it is completely out of reach.

My girls always lean into us at the end of the prayer because they expect to receive something from their mother and me. It is the same with us. God will not release what you are not expecting from Him. As it pertains to your purpose, you have to believe that God does not just want to bless you; He wants to reveal the path that He has ordered for your life to you through prayer. You cannot get so frustrated with the process that you no longer expect your purpose to be revealed.

Blind faith always leads to unlocked promises and the revelation of purpose. Praying for purpose often requires faith in something that is not yet a tangible reality. Just because you haven't seen it doesn't mean it isn't real. The moment you accept the fact that God wants to bless you, use you, and see you walking in purpose, then you can release the fear of failing by continuously walking in faithful expectation.

Trust God. Expect His best. Keep praying continuously for your purpose. As God reveals it, walk in it. Know that God always has your best interests in mind. His promises are yes and amen. Your purpose and the people connected to it are waiting. Start walking in everything God has called you to today!

PURPOSE PRAYER

Heavenly Father,

I know I was created with a purpose and that You have a plan for my life. Even when I was confused and wondered if certain things would become a reality, I thank You for never giving up on me. You are committed to my purpose and I am committed to walk in what You have created me for.

I declare that my best days are ahead of me. I declare that my purpose will be fulfilled daily as I walk according to Your Word and will. I declare that all of my ways are committed to You and that I have an expectation for You to reveal every step on my path to purpose. I declare that I do not know it all, but I am led by the One Who created it all. I declare that my purpose shall be continually fulfilled and revealed all the days of my life!

In Jesus' Name, Amen.

PURPOSE FOCUS

How often do you intentionally pray for your own purpose?

What was the last thing that you heard God say about your future? How did you respond?

Are you submitted to following all of His instructions or are you still battling with your own will?

32

Help! I Have Ants in My Pants!

MORNING MEDITATION

2 Corinthians 4:8-10

We are pressed on every side by troubles, but we are not crushed. We are perplexed, but not driven to despair. We are hunted down, but never abandoned by God. We get knocked down, but we are not destroyed. Through suffering, our bodies continue to share in the death of Jesus so that the life of Jesus may also be seen in our bodies.

EVENING DEVOTION

Galatians 2:20-22

My old self has been crucified with Christ. It is no longer I who live, but Christ lives in me. So I live in this earthly body by trusting in the Son of God, who loved me and gave himself for me. I do not treat the grace of God as meaningless. For if keeping the law could make us right with God, then there was no need for Christ to die.

Every once in a while, we send the girls to spend some special time with their PaPa (my dad). This is what we call, "warm body babysitting". We know that as long as the girls are in his presence, there is at least a warm body to monitor them without discipline. Such was the case with a recent visit.

While attending a conference in Huntsville, we received a frantic call from my dad with Layel screaming to the top of her lungs in the background. Apparently, he sent them outside to play with their cousin without his supervision. While playing, Layel stepped in an ant bed and quickly discovered the feeling of tiny ant bites up her legs. After stripping her down and applying ointment to her little legs, it seemed as if everything would be fine even beyond the tears. No allergies, no adverse repercussions.

Fast forward two weeks. We dressed the girls to prepare for family Christmas pictures, which included the girls wearing tights to accompany their skirts. After about fifteen minutes in their outfits, I hear a loud shriek from downstairs. I run down to see what the source of the issue and Layel is rolling on the floor in agony and pain. My immediate response was to look for blood and figure out how it happened. When I looked, however, there was nothing to be found. So I inquired of Layel the reason for her tears. Her reply was violently screaming, "Help! I have ants in my pants!"

After 30 minutes of reasoning with her the impossibilities of this being the case, the only way I could soothe her was to get some rubbing alcohol and apply it to the areas she felt were most affected. As soon as she received her rub down, the tears immediately stopped, and she echoed to me how much the application of the alcohol made her feel better. In my head, I was curious if ants crept in the house. At the end of my private mulling, I knew the true answer and response.

It is amazing how one painful experience can scar and wound our perception of our future. One bad relationship, without the steps of healing, has the capability of wounding every relationship we have later in life. The absence of a father or male role model, unchecked, can forever thwart our perception of men and their roles in our lives. Even one bad church experience not properly examined and healed from can transform the way we see the God who loves us beyond our deficiencies. It is never enough to simply settle for having a bad experience without digging into the trenches for healing to be released over our lives from the thing that hurt us most.

So how do you truly know that you have healed from a painful place? The truest sentiment of healing is your ability to relive or revisit the same situation with your heart being exempt from the pain that it initially imposed. The truth is, people often revisit places of hurt with the desire to subconsciously relive the pain to justify present actions. True healing, however, gives you the ability to go back to the place where the wound may have been, visit and speak about the scar, but not the reopen wound. When we truly believe the God of creation's desire to see us healed from every painful place, we will walk in His consistent love and allow that to be the place of true deliverance from what was. Even more, Psalm 103:2-3 reminds us, "Let all that I am praise the Lord; may I never forget the good things he does for me. He forgives all my sins and heals all my diseases." The Lord is the Healer of all of your wounds! He desires for His love to be the balm that brings the healing that changes you from the inside out. When you accept His healing, He gives you the power to recover in the same place where many thought they would leave you for dead. Though healing often happens in stages, it all begins with knowing the One who can change it all in a matter of moments.

There is still one important issue to weigh: though your experience may have been real, it cannot become the framework for every future interaction in your life. For Layel, the fact that she had something covering her legs for the first time since the "Ant Incident," it triggered her need for consolation beyond reason. That did not truly merit her situation. Here is the place that, if you truly let it, will transform your place of healing. You cannot expect people to apologize for a pain they didn't impose on you. Holding your future hostage because of the pain from your yesterday only limits God's ability to send people into your life who can help love your pain away.

Layel's ant bites were real, but the memory was more painful than the experience. The incident lasted less than two minutes, but her memory kept her bound to an idea of her pain that transcended the true issue at hand. For you, it may have been one season of your life, but it isn't the sum of your life. One bad season cannot be the metric by which you measure your entire lifetime. The quicker you recover from the one, the sooner you can walk into the fullness of everything God has for your future. Resist the urge to allow one challenge to hold your future hostage. Help has come, healing has been released, and the ants are no longer in your pants. Heal, forgive, and move forward.

PURPOSE PRAYER

Heavenly Father,

My life has been riddled and crippled with experiences that I wish I could have avoided. Yet in the midst of them all, I have consistently found you to be God in them. You have always proved Yourself as trustworthy. Help me, even with the pain that I felt, to not measure Your ability to heal me by the pain that once was.

I declare that my pain will not cause me to miss my future and my promise. I declare that I will daily choose to walk in the power of your healing over my life. I declare my memories will not cause me to miss the plan and destiny that You declared over my life from the foundation of the world. I declare I am healed and daily I am becoming better than I have ever been before.

In Jesus' Name, Amen.

PURPOSE FOCUS

How have painful memories kept you from moving forward in your purpose and promise?

How are you still validating your yesterday while robbing your tomorrow of what God has in store?

Have you allowed your scars to serve as a tool of your survival or a crutch to prevent you from walking forward?

Broken, but Available 33

MORNING MEDITATION

Psalm 51:16-19

You do not desire a sacrifice, or I would offer one. You do not want a burnt offering. The sacrifice you desire is a broken spirit. You will not reject a broken and repentant heart, O God. Look with favor on Zion and help her; rebuild the walls of Jerusalem. Then you will be pleased with sacrifices offered in the right spirit– with burnt offerings and whole burnt offerings. Then bulls will again be sacrificed on your altar.

EVENING DEVOTION

Jeremiah 18:1-6

The Lord gave another message to Jeremiah. He said, "Go down to the potter's shop, and I will speak to you there." So I did as he told me and found the potter working at his wheel. But the jar he was making did not turn out as he had hoped, so he crushed it into a lump of clay again and started over. Then the Lord gave me this message: "O Israel, can I not do to you as this potter has done to his clay? As the clay is in the potter's hand, so are you in my hand.

My children are notorious for breaking electronics - namely iPads, iPhones, and any other number of Apple products. I wish that I could place a number or financial value on the number of devices that I have replaced over the past five years. Many of the breaks were because of the lack of protection on the devices, which consequently led to shattered screens, dented casings, and numerous other challenges to prevent proper usage.

Most recently, Phineka - with the assistance of Layel - shattered the screen on her iPhone. This was the fourth phone broken in a two-year time span. Instead of replacing it immediately, I decided I was going into full protest mode and refused to purchase another one. I watched her learn how to text and navigate through her apps without slicing her finger on fractures of the screen. When she would talk on the phone, she would use the speaker function instead of placing the phone on her cheek to prevent shards of glass from entering her face. I watched all this while my pristine phone without any damage continued to function normally.

One Saturday afternoon, we went to Bath and Body Works to use some online coupons that she had been begging to use. We filled two separate bags with soaps, lotions, etc. and once we arrived at the counter, I laughed at her because her phone would be needed to scan the coupons. As we approached two different cashiers to check out, something happened that I was not expecting. My phone wouldn't scan! The cashier tried numerous times without success.

The frustrating part, however, was not that my phone refused to scan. It was when I looked over to my right and watched as the cashier seamlessly scanned Phineka's phone time after time for every coupon she had. There wasn't one glitch in the system or lack of ability because of the cracks and dents in her phone. Instead, despite the damage that was on the face of the device, the functionality and purpose were still readily used and available.

Most of us wait until "we" feel like we are healed enough to gain the posture of complete surrender to God. We diagnose the areas where we are weakest, where we have been broken, where life has left us for dead and trampled upon us without grace. We remember each pit we've fallen in by name and use all of these deficiencies as a disqualification from being used by God. The truth of the matter, however, has less to do with how bad we view the damage and more to do with the God of all grace and sufficiency covering our shortcomings with His strength.

Though we can never overlook the challenges that life has dealt us, what we can learn is that God always asks for one thing in the midst of them: our availability. I often look at it from the perspective of Jesus, battered and bruised, carrying the cross up Calvary's hill. In that position, He was broken and torn, fatigued and fighting the temptation to call a legion of angels to save Him from the misery of death. In the midst of His brokenness, He stood available to be used. The stress and strain of the moment did not usurp His ability to stand ready for God's purpose.

When we magnify our brokenness over the prevailing strength that we find in Christ during the moments of our greatest deficiencies, we create a crutch than enables our issues instead of delivering us through the power of the experience. Broken should be something that transpires over a season or a moment, not something that becomes the identifying trait of your character and your entire life. When you refuse to stay broken, you invite the power of the Almighty God to bring your heart to a place of healing.

So how does that transpire? In the moments of your greatest brokenness, God is not looking for you to mend your pieces. Simply put, He is looking for you to be available. Not having it all together in your own eyes is not an excuse to keep the Potter from making you into what He has designed you to be. Time after time, I have watched God take the messiest of lives and turn them into beautiful masterpieces. Whenever you leave your life in the hands of the One who created it, He can take fractures and splintered pieces and develop something greater than anyone could have ever imagined.

In reality, brokenness is a state of mind and not a state of life. When you make the conscious decision to place your hands back in the hands of the One who knows you best, He can take your little and make you better than you could have ever dreamed. Don't hide in your brokenness. Be available in it.

PURPOSE PRAYER

Heavenly Father,

I have been marred by own brokenness and crippled by my inability to get things moving in the right direction. I have tried it my way and fail every time. Today, I want completely yield by deficiencies to You and trust that You will make up the difference in every area of my life.

I declare that I am not my mistake, but I am the workmanship of an Almighty God created to do great exploits in His name. I declare that the pain of my memories will not stop the promise of my future. I declare that even in my most challenging state, my life will remain available to the God of all creation to work a miracle on my behalf.

In Jesus Name, Amen.

PURPOSE FOCUS

How have you allowed your deficiencies to speak up for you too soon? Have you been your own crutch preventing purpose from being released in your life?

What would it take for you to make your life completely available to God?

How committed are you to allowing God to heal your heart not just by words and actions, but by His unfailing love?

34

It Wasn't Me!

MORNING MOTIVATION

Romans 8:1-4

So now there is no condemnation for those who belong to Christ Jesus.[2] And because you belong to him, the power of the life-giving Spirit has freed you from the power of sin that leads to death. [3] The law of Moses was unable to save us because of the weakness of our sinful nature. So God did what the law could not do. He sent his own Son in a body like the bodies we sinners have. And in that body God declared an end to sin's control over us by giving his Son as a sacrifice for our sins. [4] He did this so that the just requirement of the law would be fully satisfied for us, who no longer follow our sinful nature but instead follow the Spirit.

EVENING DEVOTION

Romans 12:9-11

This great dragon—the ancient serpent called the devil, or Satan, the one deceiving the whole world—was thrown down to the earth with all his angels. [10] Then I heard a loud voice shouting across the heavens, "It has come a last salvation and power and the Kingdom of our God, and the authority of his Christ. For the accuser of our brothers and sisters has been thrown down to earth— the one who accuses them before our God day and night. [11] And they have defeated him by the blood of the Lamb and by their testimony. And they did not love their lives so much that they were afraid to die.

Layel, who is now very active and energetic, has become the master of the trade when it comes to iPads. It is as if she came out of the womb with supreme iPad mastery skills. She can work it better than

Phineka with a follow-up explanation and analysis of what she is doing. Some days it is downright baffling to watch her methodically jump from app to app with her legs crossed in her bed or on the couch. Other days, it's downright annoying.

The issue that I began to run into happened at the hands of this amazing child. Each morning, I do a devotional and time of prayer on Periscope. I intentionally leave my iPad wherever I recorded the video. One morning, I got up and frantically began to search for my device. It wasn't where I left it last...it wasn't in my book bag...it wasn't even on my side of the bed. When the iPad was finally discovered hours later, it was nestled underneath Layel's covers dead as a doorknob.

This trend continued for several days, even weeks. I would go to look for my device, and it would be nowhere to be found. Then suddenly, Layel would appear with my device with the power meter below 5% every time. It became a game to her and a nuisance to me. She finally arrived at the point where she would bring it to me before the end of the night so I would at least know where it was... even if the power had been completely drained.

One particular morning, I woke up extremely late for my morning devotion and hurried down the stairs. When I looked for my device, it was gone again. I jumped on my phone and began my recording by ranting to the watchers about how Layel had taken my iPad again. This particular morning, Londyn woke up in the middle of my broadcast and joined me downstairs. As I wrapped up the recording, I decided to rant once again to my followers about Layel taking my iPad. Londyn said, "Daddy, Layel didn't take it. Ashriel did. She's using it as an alarm clock." Unconvinced, I woke Layel up and asked her where my iPad was. She proudly exclaimed, "It wasn't me!" Sure enough, the device was in Ashriel's room. My apologies quickly filled the ears of my little one as I learned a very valuable lesson.

Isn't it amazing how you can live your life out of God's will for so long that when you finally decide to make a change, everyone still holds you to your old standard? It's easy for them to charge your present without merit since they were privy to the mistakes of your past.

The beauty of walking in purpose and coming into the full knowledge of God's will for your life is knowing that though you have a history, it cannot and will not be the basis and definition of your future! Sure, you've made mistakes and participated in actions that you wish you could take back. However, on this side of the cross, God has cast your sin as far as the east is from the west. He no longer holds you captive by your mistakes and decisions of yesteryear. Despite your mistakes, He continues to push you to pursue everything He has created you to accomplish.

You cannot run the risk of being a martyr to your history and consequently refusing to fulfill what God created you to do! Your new confession, even in the face of your greatest adversities, must be, "It wasn't me!" Back then, you may have been the one to follow down that erroneous path. Now that you have been set free, the stains of guilt no longer blemish your life. Pursue purpose without the fear of not being loved and accepted by a God who knew your mistakes before you ever made them! You are no longer bound but forever free!

This freedom comes with a price. Unmerited accusations may come, but you must resist the temptation to fall back into bondage. Your aim should always be to walk in the complete knowledge of your newfound freedom in Christ. Let them accuse you, but live above reproach as you passionately pursue purpose. Though you may have been guilty, the beauty of knowing Christ is being able to say boldly and clearly, "It wasn't me!" He paid the price, washed you clean, and covered you in the power of His blood. Now chase Him - not those who hold your history over your head.

PURPOSE PRAYER

Heavenly Father,

Thank you for forgiving me of every sin I have ever committed. My life deserved the penalty that it was preparing to receive. Instead, you took my judgement so that I could walk in the purpose you created me for. Thank you for making me innocent when guilt was what I deserved. I declare that I will spend the rest of my life pursuing your created purpose for my life. I declare that my history will never had the power to retain me in bondage. I declare that my freedom has been purchased at a price that merits my life surrender. I will look to You forever and not at the mistakes I made. I did it, but You declared, "It wasn't me!"

In Jesus' Name, Amen.

PURPOSE FOCUS

Have you learned how to live above the accusations of people?

How do you respond when people bring up your past? Are you still living under condemnation and unforgiveness?

Are you fully aware of the grace that has been poured out on your life so that you can walk in your purpose and not condemnation?

35

Starting Over

MORNING MOTIVATION

2 Timothy 1:6-7

This is why I remind you to fan into flames the spiritual gift God gave you when I laid my hands on you. For God has not given us a spirit of fear and timidity, but of power, love, and self-discipline.

EVENING DEVOTION

Isaiah 43:18-19

"But forget all that– it is nothing compared to what I am going to do. For I am about to do something new. See, I have already begun! Do you not see it? I will make a pathway through the wilderness. I will create rivers in the dry wasteland.

May 2016 became a major tipping point and place of transition for my family. After spending five years in the desert and enjoying leading an amazing church, we knew that the time had come for us to make our transition out of the West and closer to home. It honestly was the hardest decision in the life of our young family. When we moved to Tucson, all of our children were pretty young. In essence, all they knew was Arizona. We knew that when it came time to share the news with them, it would be the most difficult part of the process.

I'll never forget the evening we all sat on the couch in our living room as I shared the news of our transition. I tried to use every selling point I could find - from being closer to their "Poppa T" and family to having the benefit of all four seasons of the year. When I looked into their little eyes, I could see the tears quickly swelling as the fear of leaving familiarity and walking into uncertainty filled their hearts.

As they opened their mouths, they questioned everything. "Where will we live? What about our friends? What about our current church? Are you being fired? Why would you leave now? Could we hold off another couple years? Do we have to go?" The questions were countless. They came from a sincere place embedded in their hearts. Tucson was all they knew. The threat of walking away from that almost paralyzed them to regret the words even came out of my mouth.

Fast-forward six months. As we continuously work through the stages of settling in and making Georgia our home, the biggest change has happened in the lives of my little humans. One day, as we were making one of our weekly voyages into the city, Ashriel blurted these words out of the blue: "I didn't know I could be as happy as I am in another city." Londyn quickly chimed in, "I love our new house, my new school, and my new friends...I just hate having to drive so far to get everywhere." Amana echoed, "We get to see Poppa all the time now!" Even Layel, who has no real concept of the depth of transitions, mimicked the words of her sisters. You see, if we had allowed the fear of starting over rob us of the opportunity at hand, we would have never known what was waiting in front of us.

All too often, fear becomes the controlling mechanism that paralyzes destinies and futures. It is the fear of the unknown – having to courageously walk into something that is uncertain and unclear – that causes people to second-guess the God that calls them out of their comfort zone and into His promises. Whenever fear controls us, faith is silenced. Wherever faith has been forced to surrender the reigns of your destiny, comfortability quickly sinks in and keeps you at a standstill in your purpose. Stagnation is just like quicksand. It only tries to controls you when you attempt to move away from it. The longer you allow fear to control you, the longer you are robbed of the bright future on the other side of your discomfort.

No matter how many failures your life has seen, you can never be afraid to start all over again. Just because life happened to you and kept you from excelling at the level or degree that you originally intended does not mean that has to be your testimony forever. We are faced with ditches, potholes, and unexpected "happenings" that have the ability to thwart our progress and render us powerless. In the midst of feeling powerless, there is a Power at work in us that silences our fear and grants us the grace to move forward in strength and authority. It is this strength that makes monotony spring to life again and causes victory to be mantled on our lives.

If fear can rob you of the ability to start over, you will forever be a prisoner to your present state. You will always envision your hopes and dreams as mere impossibilities. So many people have gone to the grave with destiny locked away on the inside of them simply because they were afraid to start over again. Even God started over again with humanity through the life of Noah (Genesis 6). Starting over is not a sin, but coveting the life of someone who took a chance while you could take the same opportunity is.

Today, make the conscious decision to refuse to allow your yesterday to rule your tomorrow. Life may have happened to you, but now is your opportunity to make it happen for you. Take the mistakes and mishaps you have experienced and use them as the catapult to push you forward. It may not be easy, but it will be beyond worth it.

PURPOSE PRAYER

Heavenly Father,

Thank you for giving me the strength to begin again. My life has been riddled with my own personal miscues, but thank You for the grace to start again. My imperfections and insecurities have never put you in fear. You have loved me and embraced me just as I am and for that, I'm thankful.
I declare that I will be delivered from the spirit of fear and walk wholeheartedly in the power of Your love. I declare that my history is not my future me and I will become all that You created me for. I declare that familiarity will not stop me from bringing to life all that you put on the inside of me. This reset is just the beginning of the greatness that will unfold in my life!

In Jesus' Name, Amen.

PURPOSE FOCUS

What has paralyzed you from starting over again?

If money was not a hindrance, what would you spend the rest of your life doing? How can you begin that process today?

How can God use even your mistakes to push your purpose as you start over again?

STAY CONNECTED

Thank you for purchasing the Special Edition of Daddy, Daughters, and Devotions. LaBryant would like to stay connected with you! Here are a few ways you can stay updated on new book releases, speaking engagements, ministry events, and more!

FACEBOOK LaBryant Friend
INSTAGRAM @labryantfriend
PERISCOPE @labryantfriend
WEBSITE www.labryantfriend.com